Computerised Accounting Using

Sage

NVQ 2 and 3

Bryan Barnsley

Before entering the teaching profession Bryan Barnsley spent more than 30 years in accounting and management positions in both industry and commerce. Since 1986 he has been a lecturer in Business Studies at Tamworth College in Staffordshire. In his current position he is responsible for co-ordinating the HND/HNC courses in Business and Finance, and the small business courses. Bryan also continues to run his own small family business which keeps him in touch with developments in the business world and helps in his activities as a business counsellor.

DP Publications Ltd
Aldine Place, London W12 8AW
1994

Acknowledgements

I would like to thank everyone who helped contribute to this courseware from the idea stage to the finished product. Particularly Pamela Whitehouse and Doreen Wells for their involvement in the early stages of the project

In particular we would like to thank:

The Banking Information Service, who have kindly given their permission for us to use specimen cheques and other material provided by them.

The countless students at Tamworth College who have evaluated earlier versions.

Lecturers in Colleges of Further Education in Staffordshire who have used and evaluated an earlier version, and whose comments and suggestions have influenced the structure and content of this courseware.

All companies and persons named in this book are purely ficticious, with the exception of those named in the samples provided by the Banking Information Service, and any likeness to any real person or company is coincidental.

A CIP catalogue record for this book is available from the British Library

ISBN 1 85805 087 1
Copyright © Bryan Barnsley 1994
First Edition 1994

Typeset by Kai Typesetting, Nottingham

Printed by in Great Britain by the Guernsey Press Co Ltd, Vale, Guernsey CI

Preface

Aim

The aim of this book is to provide students with the material for a practical introduction to computerised accounting, using the popular accounting package Sage, to the level of competency required for NVQ 2 and 3 in Accounting.

It is intended for two **separate** groups of students:

a)   Those who already have an understanding of manual methods of accounting and wish to learn how tasks can be performed using a computer. Such students are likely to be on Small Business Training schemes, or similar courses.

   They should need to work through Part 1 of the book only (see *Approach* below).

b)   Those who are learning the principles of bookkeeping and accounts, and need to appreciate how accounts may be kept by both manual and computerised methods. Such students are likely to be on GNVQ Business Studies Intermediate or Advanced, or AAT courses aiming at NVQ 2 and 3 Accounting competency.

   They will need to work through Part 2 of the book (see *Approach* below).

Need

There is a great deal of material available on accounting and bookkeeping principles, but very little inexpensive material that enables students to gain competence in the practical skills of performing accounting tasks using a computer. This book aims to fill this gap.

Approach

The units in this book are centred around a small wholesale company called Family Favourites. The company makes both cash and credit sales and, like most small companies when starting up, has been operating a manual accounting system until a computerised system can be justified or afforded. This time has now arrived, and the company has purchased a Sage computerised accounting system.

The Sage Sterling Range can provide considerable management control information, such as analysis by area and product, cost analysis of products, minimum order value reports and variance analysis. However, this book starts at the point when Family Favourites is just beginning to transfer its manual accounting system to a Sage computerised system.

Part 1 – Setting up and using a computerised accounting system

Part 1 of the book is a self-contained course on computerised accounting using Sage. It is organised as a series of progressive units, and the assumption is that the student will start at the first unit and work through to the last.

- ❑ Units 1 to 7 cover the setting up of ledgers and processing of a month's transactions, and can be treated as a single block to show the basic ledger operations.

- ❑ Units 8 to 11 cover end-of-month adjustments for Unit 12 in which a Trading and Profit and Loss Account and Balance sheet are produced.

- ❑ Units 13 enables comparisons with budgets.

- ❑ Units 14 to 18 process a further month's transactions, and introduce automatic invoicing and linking to stock control.

- ❑ Unit 19 covers the production of VAT returns, and Unit 20 shows how a variety of month-end reports and management reports can be generated.

- ❑ The Payroll Section deals, as suggested by the title, with a payroll system.

- ❑ At the end of Part 1 is the December 1993 IAB exam paper for the Diploma in Computerised Bookkeeping, the contents of which is covered in Units 1–20.

Satisfactory completion of Units 1–20 can be used as evidence of competence for NVQ Level 3 Accounting.

Part 2 – Processing accounting information manually and then transferring it to a computerised system

Part 2 consists of a number of units which **combine** manual methods with computerised methods. The units are intended to be worked through progressively from first to last.

Each unit in Part 2 first directs the student to produce manual records, and then directs him or her to the appropriate units in Part 1 to transfer the records onto the computerised system. In this way, the student can clearly see the differences between a manual and a computerised system and thus better appreciate the advantages of computerisation.

Answers to the tasks for manual production of records for the first month's transactions are provided in an appendix in order to:

a)   highlight where students may falter on principles of accounting, and

b)   enable comparisons with computerised results.

Satisfactory completion of units 1 to 5 can be used as evidence of competence for NVQ Level 2 Accounting, and units 6 and 8 for NVQ Level 3 Accounting.

Note for lecturers

Whether your students work through Part 1 of the book only, or through the whole of the book as directed from within Part 2, they will need one disk on which to build their files and data. This avoids duplication of work as, while the students work through the units, the files and data are stored for later re-use.

As part of the lecturers' supplement (see below) you are provided with a disk containing the files at critical stages for your own use, ie after Units 1 and 2, Unit 8, Unit 13, Unit 17 and Unit 18. You may use these for a variety of purposes, but principally they will help prevent the need for students who damage their disks, for whatever reason, to re-input data.

Appendix – Solutions to manual January calculations

This contains the solutions to the manual January transactions in Part 2.

Using the Payroll II system

The Sage Payroll II program is an easy-to-use comprehensive payroll program. It will automatically calculate the requirements for PAYE, National Insurance, Statutory Sick Pay, Statutory Maternity Pay, and cater for changes in government legislation.

Apart form the normal payroll requirements the program allows you to store and summarise all the payment details for the tax year end.

What hardware and software do you need?

Students will need access to an IBM or IBM compatible PC with two floppy disk drives or a hard disk.

The software needed is the Sage Sterling Range, preferably Accountant, Accountant Plus, or Financial Controller, although many of the exercises can be used with Bookkeeper. To use the Payroll Supplement, additional software is needed – Sage Payroll II.

What this book does not do

The book is not a general introduction to the use of microcomputers; it assumes some prior knowledge of and familiarity with the use of microcomputer applications.

It will not tell users how to install the Sage programs. You will need to refer to your software manual for this, and you may need some technical help with installation.

Using an integrated accounting system

The Sterling Range of programs is a truly integrated accounting system. All the functions are included for a fully automated sales, purchases and nominal ledger system, together with a comprehensive range of reports.

The bookkeeping functions have been simplified by standardising many of the operations and routines. All ledgers and control accounts are automatically updated with only one keyboard entry.

From the program it is easy to produce aged analyses of creditors and debtors, monthly day books, bank details, the VAT return, monthly and year-to-date profit and loss accounts, balance sheets and budget comparisons, and many other useful reports.

Lecturers' Supplement

This is supplied free of charge to those lecturers using the book as a course text. It contains the answers to the February transactions that the students are required to complete manually in Part 2. There is also a 3½" disk containing files at critical stages of the computerised accounting procedures (see *Note for lecturers* above).

Bryan Barnsley
April 1994

Contents

Part 2 Processing accounting information manually and then transferring it to a computerised system

Part 1: Setting up and using a computerised accounting system

Introduction

This part of the book details the first steps in setting up and using a computerised accounting system which could become the centre of the company's management control system. Completion of units 1–20 can be used as evidence of competence for NVQ 3 Accounting.

You should work through this part in sequence, retaining the files you create on disk for subsequent use.

Note: If you wish to understand how a manual system would deal with the transactions you should work through Part 2 of this book.

Contents

Getting started

Firstly, it is necessary to set up your computer.

Using a hard disk

Please refer to your Sage Accountant Plus Manual for installation and startup, then follow the instructions from number 4 below.

Tutors and students in colleges where a hard disk machine is used may need to obtain help from the technician to get started.

Using floppy disks

LOAD AND RUN

1. Switch on the machine
2. Insert MS-DOS disk
3. At A> remove DOS disk and insert the Sage Program disk
4. Type SAGE (Enter)

The program will ask for the date

5. Enter today's date (Enter)
6. The password is LETMEIN (Enter)

The program will ask for a data disk in drive **B**

7. Insert a blank, formatted data disk into B (Enter)

The program is now displaying the main menu, shown below, and ready to run.

SAGE MENU PROGRAM

```
+--------------------------------------+
|                                      |
|        MAIN MENU                     |
|                                      |
|        Sales Ledger                  |
|        Purchase Ledger               |
|        Nominal Ledger                |
|        Payroll                       |
|        Stock Control                 |
|        Sales Order Processing        |
|        Report Generator Utilities    |
|        Quit                          |
|                                      |
+--------------------------------------+
```

To move around the Main Menu use the arrow keys on the number pad, or the Home and End Keys. When you are positioned over a menu item you want to select, press ENTER.

Should you wish to finish **always select Quit** from the Main Menu; this will ensure that all your data has been saved on the data disk.

If you make an incorrect selection from any of the menus, you can always return to the previous menu by pressing the Escape Key (Esc).

Unit 1: Initialisation

Before you can begin to process any accounts data, blank data files have to be created. An initialisation routine creates the necessary space for each ledger account. The first task then is to decide how many accounts will be required in each of the Sales, Purchase and Nominal ledgers.

Nominal accounts define the different types of sales and purchase categories and overhead or expense categories (i.e. rent, salaries etc.).

Accounts in the Sales Ledger will tell you how much has been invoiced to or paid by a customer.

Accounts in the Purchase Ledger will tell you how much your firm has been invoiced or how much you have paid a supplier.

A time will come when there is no more space on the disk and at this stage you will have to run the reconfiguration routine. This allows you to remove unwanted transactions i.e. invoices that have been fully paid, from the data files thereby creating more space for additional transactions.

Having loaded the program as described on page 3:

> Choose UTILITIES from the Menu
> Choose DATA FILE UTILITIES
> Choose DATA FILE CHANGES
> Choose REBUILD DATA FILES
> Select LEDGER FILES

1.1 Setting up the records

Enter the appropriate values alongside the prompts

Number of Sales accounts	50
Number of Purchase Accounts	50
Number of Nominal Accounts	100

Press RETURN to continue and you will be asked

Do you have any existing data?

Enter NO

1.2 Setting up the control accounts

Do you want the existing Nominal Ledger Default structure?

Enter YES

The program will set up the Nominal Ledger Accounts.

At this stage it is advisable to enter any VAT RATES CHANGES.

1.3 Entering VAT

Choose VAT/TAX code changes.

VAT Rate 0   relates to Zero rated Items such as food, books, newspapers and childrens' clothes

VAT Rate 1   is the Standard Rate which applies to most goods and services

VAT Rate 2   applies to exempt goods and services which would include insurance, rent, training and education VAT Rates 3-8 are available for any additional separate rates which could be introduced

VAT Rate 9   is reserved for transactions not subject to VAT such as Journal Entries and Transfers

The VAT rates can be altered to cater for the current legislation

With your arrow keys move to VAT Rate 1 and overtype with the current rate 17.5% and ENTER. This must be entered on each line under rate 1 by moving your arrow down the screen.

After completion press ESC and go back to the Sage Menu Program.

Unit 2: Setting up the Nominal Accounts

2.1 To create Nominal Ledger Accounts

The program already has a default nominal coding system which can usually be modified for your requirements. Family Favourites decide to adopt this system with the following modifications.

To print out the default Nominal Accounts List:

Choose NOMINAL LEDGER from the menu
Choose ACCOUNTS LIST
Lower account reference ....[Enter]
Upper account reference ....[Enter]
Display print or file.................................[Print]

Press ENTER to produce the accounts list.

Now alter it as follows:

Choose NOMINAL ACCOUNT STRUCTURE
Choose ACCOUNT NAMES
Choose account reference 2330 ....[Enter]
Overtype account name ....[WAGES CONTROL]

Escape and Post and repeat for the following codes:
(If it is a new account enter [YES])

3000	ORDINARY SHARES
4000	SALES CLOTHES
4001	SALES SPORTSWEAR
4002	SALES HOUSEHOLD
4950	OPENING STOCK CLOTHES
4951	OPENING STOCK SPORTSWEAR
4952	OPENING STOCK HOUSEHOLD
5000	PURCHASES CLOTHES
5001	PURCHASES SPORTSWEAR
5002	PURCHASE HOUSEHOLD
5200	CLOSING STOCK CLOTHES
5201	CLOSING STOCK SPORTSWEAR
5202	CLOSING STOCK HOUSEHOLD
8200	ADVERTISING
9998	SUSPENSE ACCOUNT
6201	[DELETE] THIS ITEM

After you have entered all of these codes, press ESCAPE (Esc) again and return to the Sub-Menu.

Go to NOMINAL ACCOUNTS LIST and enter (P) to print a list of Nominal Ledger Codes.

Keep this printout to refer to as you will need to refer to it constantly to code all your transactions.

2.2 Setting up the Purchase and Sales Ledgers

Whenever a purchase or sale is made on credit it is necessary to update the appropriate account in the Sales or Purchase Ledger.

Accounts in these ledgers have a reference which consists of up to six characters – either numbers or letters. There are no special rules on how to choose a reference, but you should use a convention and style that will be consistent and therefore easy to remember, eg:

Sagesoft Ltd. could simply be SAGE
British Telecom could be BT
Wheelers Garage could be WHEEL

When setting up the purchase and sales ledgers, make a list of the names of all your customers and suppliers and create a reference for each of them, then record their name and address on the Ledger diskette.

2.3 To enter details of new customers

Choose SALES LEDGER from the Main Menu
Choose CUSTOMER DETAILS from the Sub-Menu

You will be asked the following question:

> *Account Reference?*

Enter the reference you have chosen for the customer/supplier, e.g. [WHITBY].

The system checks to see that this reference has not already been used and, if it is unused, will ask you to confirm that you wish to create a new account by asking:

> *Is this a new account?*

You will answer [YES].

If you have entered the wrong account reference answer [NO] and you will be asked to re-enter the reference number.

You should now enter the appropriate name and address alongside each of the relevant prompts. See additional information for Credit Limits under Units 2.5 and 2.6.

CUSTOMERS ACCOUNT (SALES LEDGER)

J. Whitby, Homeleigh, Tamworth Rd., Amington, Tamworth.	WHITBY
T. Blankley, 5 Ingold Ave, Walsall.	BLANK
A. Holloway, The Fairings, Four Oaks, West Midlands.	HOLLO
J. Williams, 3 The Avenue, Polesworth, Tamworth.	WILLI
H. Whitehouse, 26 Thorne Rd., Sutton Coldfield.	WHITE
P. Weir, 32 Cedar Rd., Cannock, Staffs.	WEIR
J. Goldingay, 71 Chiltern Rd., Wolverhampton.	GOLD
M. Harris, Sevenoaks, Long Lane, Lichfield, Staffs.	HARRIS
C. Evans, 42 Oak View, Rugeley, Staffs.	EVANS
A. Nolan, 14 Hatherton St., Cheslyn Hay, West Midlands.	NOLAN

On completion press ESCAPE [Esc] and return to the Main Menu.

If a customer or supplier changes his address at a later date then you will come back to this option, enter the appropriate reference and make any adjustments to the existing data.

> Now choose ADDRESS LIST from the main menu,
> LOWER ACCOUNT REFERENCE, UPPER ACCOUNT REFERENCE,
> NAMES OR ADDRESS, DISPLAY OR PRINT and enter P to print out a list of Customers Names. This will be needed for processing Sales Invoices.

2.4 To enter details of new suppliers

> Choose PURCHASE LEDGER from the Main Menu
> Choose SUPPLIER DETAILS from the Sub-Menu

You will be asked similar questions to those you were asked when entering details of new customers.

SUPPLIERS ACCOUNTS (PURCHASE LEDGER)

Levis, 3 Broad St., Birmingham.	LEVI
Britannia, Unit 4, Green Lane, Cannock, Staffs.	BRITN
Mann Richards, Unit 6, Green Lane, Cannock, Staffs.	MRICH
Nikey, 75 London Rd., Leicester.	NIKE
Betterwares, 7 Sutton Way, Sutton Coldfield, West Mids.	BETTER
Racquets & Balls, 26 New Invention, Walsall.	RACQT

On completion press ESCAPE (Esc) and return to the Sub-Menu. Now choose ADDRESS LIST and proceed as in 2.3 and press (P) to print out a list of Suppliers Names. This will be needed for you to process Purchase Invoices.

2.5 Additional Information on Debtors and Creditors

This program allows you to keep quite a lot of information about your customers and suppliers, as shown under Units 2.6 and 2.7.

CREDIT LIMIT

If you establish credit limits for any of your customers or if a credit limit has been fixed by your supplier you can enter this value within this option. On the Account History, Aged Debtors/Creditors and Statements the current balance will be compared with the credit limit and a warning message printed if the credit limit has been exceeded.

TURNOVER

The turnover will be accumulated whenever you enter an invoice or credit note for each account. This value will be shown on the Aged Debtors/Creditors reports and can be used to see which are your best customer/suppliers. You can use this option to enter an existing value if you are starting your accounts during a financial year.

TELEPHONE NUMBER AND CONTACT NAME

The name and number will be printed on Aged Debtors/Creditors report so that you can telephone suppliers/customers immediately to sort out any overdue balances.

SORT CODE

You can enter any alphanumeric characters you like to represent area code, product group, salespersons, etc. This can then be used in the Report Generator to assist selection of specific accounts, e.g. a report consisting of all sales in the Midlands – area code.

ANALYSIS CODE

This can be used to record VAT registration numbers or area codes etc.

2.6 Suppliers information

We will now add extra information about our suppliers.

> Select PURCHASE LEDGER from the Main Menu
> Select SUPPLIER DETAILS from the Sub-Menu

Use your reference number to access the appropriate accounts and add the extra details:

NAME	CREDIT	TEL. NO.	CONTACT NAME	VAT REG.
Betterwares	2500	0922 4545	Mr B Anker	343 5646 99
Britannia	1500	0902 3421	Mr E Fox	644 7353 34
Levis	5000	0854 4315	Mrs S Miles	453 9459 94
Mann Rich	4000	0394 4134	Ms J Lee	486 9459 94
Nikey	4500	9483 2389	Mrs G Holt	842 4294 34
Racquets & Balls	3400	4832 2842	Ms P Holland	384 4985 09

2.7 Customer information

Now access the Sales ledger and enter the following information in the CUSTOMER DETAILS.

NAME	CREDIT	TEL. NO.	CONTACT NAME	VAT REG.
Whitby	2400	0342 2428	Mrs J Whitby	959 3493 83
Blankley	1500	4833 4242	Mrs T Blankley	424 9892 43
Holloway	1000	4584 5833	Mr A Holloway	443 4842 43
Williams	1400	4838 8422	Mrs J Williams	482 8482 55
Whitehouse	1500	4842 8284	Mrs H Whitehouse	842 8935 43
Weir	1400	3483 4384	Mr P Weir	347 3242 34
Goldingay	2000	4932 5677	Miss J Goldingay	456 7635 45
Harris	2500	4932 7654	Mrs M Harris	243 5435 43
Evans	2750	3433 7653	Mrs C Evans	424 4244 43
Nolan	2250	9094 5222	Mrs A Nolan	838 8483 43

When you have completed your invoice postings you will be able to look at the Aged Debtors/Creditors to see if any of our customers have exceeded their credit limit, or if we have exceeded our credit limit with suppliers.

Unit 3: Opening Balances

Always start your computerised accounting on the first day of a month.

On the day at which you decide to start entering transactions you will be owed money by some of your customers and you will owe money to your suppliers for earlier invoices that have not been paid; these are called OPENING BALANCES.

A decision will have to be made as to whether or not you wish to enter the current outstanding balance as one single entry, or to enter all the individual invoices that are outstanding.

The latter is recommended since it will make it easier to allocate payments later on, (especially if cash discounts are involved) and also to look at aged reports.

3.1 Debtors Opening Balance

To enter details for Customers who owe you money:

> Choose SALES LEDGER from the Main Menu
> Choose BATCHED DATA ENTRY from the Sub-Menu
> Choose SALES INVOICES

Type in the opening balances (details shown below) using Opening Balance for the detail and post to the SUSPENSE ACCOUNT, nominal code 9998.

Since these transactions do not involve VAT the tax code will be T9. If a customer's account is in credit you enter the opening balance under CREDIT NOTES from the Sub-Menu.

Note: Where there are two entries for the same customer, eg Harris, this means that the customer has been invoiced for goods on two separate occasions.

DEBTORS OPENING BALANCES NOMINAL CODE=9998

To repeat this code and the description press F6.

	DATE	N/C	DETAILS	£	T/C
Harris	30.11.93	9998	Opening balances	60.11	T9
Harris	12.12.93	9998	Opening balances	75.10	T9
Whitehouse	31.12.93	9998	Opening balances	86.50	T9
Williams	05.11.93	9998	Opening balances	52.00	T9
Williams	06.12.93	9998	Opening balances	50.37	T9
Nolan	31.12.93	9998	Opening balances	43.00	T9
Goldingay	16.12.93	9998	Opening balances	27.12	T9
Weir	15.12.93	9998	Opening balances	45.07	T9
Evans	30.11.93	9998	Opening balances	73.63	T9
Whitby	05.11.93	9998	Opening balances	29.17	T9
Holloway	07.12.93	9998	Opening balances	98.62	T9
Blankley	06.11.93	9998	Opening balances	134.70	T9

After entering all of the data press ESC and then the bottom of the screen will show Post, Edit or Abandon.

Check that your debtors and creditors figures agree with the trial balance under Unit 3.3. If any alteration is necessary select Edit and alter figures.

Once the figures agree select Post, [ESC] and return to the Sage Menu Program

3.2 Creditors opening balance

To enter details for suppliers who we owe money to:

> Choose PURCHASES LEDGER from the Main Menu
> Choose BATCH DATA ENTRY from the Sub-Menu
> Choose PURCHASE INVOICES

Enter as for the sales, i.e. using code 9998, VAT code T9, and entering the detail as opening balance.

You are recommended to enter individual invoices for customers separately, rather than as one figure.

CREDITORS OPENING BALANCES NOMINAL CODE=9998					
	DATE	N/C	DETAILS	£	T/C
Levis	30.11.93	9998	Opening balances	98.64	T9
Britannia	23.11.93	9998	Opening balances	404.00	T9
Racquets & Balls	05.12.93	9998	Opening balances	106.32	T9
Nikey	10.12.93	9998	Opening balances	3,521.63	T9
Mann Richards	12.12.93	9998	Opening balances	603.72	T9
Betterwares	24.12.93	9998	Opening balances	173.21	T9

After entering the Opening Purchase and Sales Ledger Balances, you need to zero these entries in the Nominal Ledger before entering the Nominal Ledger Opening Balances, otherwise the Debtors and Creditors will be duplicated. To do this (ESC) back to the Sage Menu Program

> Choose NOMINAL LEDGER
> Choose TRIAL BALANCE and Print [P]

This will give you the value of the opposite entries to cancel these figures from the Trial Balance. Now choose JOURNAL ENTRIES and enter the opposite entries, by crediting N/C 1100 and debiting N/C 2100 and crediting the Suspense Account to cancel the balance, as shown below.

Ref JNL1
Date 01/01/94

N/C	DETAILS	T/C	DEBIT	CREDIT
1100	Opposite Entries	T9		?
2100	Opposite Entries	T9	?	
9998	Opposite Entries	T9		?

Press ESC and POST

3.3 Nominal Ledger Balances

There are also other opening balances in the Nominal Ledger. These are entered via the Journal.

> Choose NOMINAL LEDGER from the Main Menu
> Choose JOURNAL ENTRIES from the Sub-Menu

Enter the date as 010194, the date we are entering the accounts from.
The ref. should be your initials or JNL 1.
Details must be opening balance. Tax code must be T9.

The cursor will now move down to the main body of the journal.

You should complete one line for each transaction. The value for each particular transaction should be entered into either the Debit column or the Credit column *not both.*

You will not be allowed to ESCAPE out of this routine until the sum of the values in the Debit column equals the sum of the values in the Credit column.

The system maintains a batch total in the top right hand corner of the screen to inform you of the difference between the two columns.

It's a good idea to write the opening entries onto a batch sheet beforehand, especially if the number of entries is going to exceed one screen. This is to make sure it balances.

From the trial balance below enter the opening entries in the journal.

FAMILY FAVOURITES TRIAL BALANCE 1/1/94

CODE	ACCOUNT	DETAIL	DR £	CR £
0011	Lease	O/Bal	10000.00	
0050	Motor Van	O/Bal	5000.00	
4950	O/stock clothes	O/Bal	1287.10	
4951	O/stock sportswear	O/Bal	1696.50	
4952	O/stock household	O/Bal	738.50	
1100	Debtors	O/Bal	775.39	
1200	Bank	O/Bal	1020.00	
2100	Creditors	O/Bal		4907.52
2210	PAYE & NI	O/Bal		75.89
2200	VAT	O/Bal		230.72
3000	Share capital	O/Bal		10000.00
3200	Profit & loss	O/Bal		5303.36
			20517.49	20517.49

IMPORTANT NOTE! Before attempting Journal entries you must make sure you have sufficient TIME to complete all the entries. This is because the program will not allow you to ESCAPE unless all Debit and Credit Balances agree.

Press ESC, check and then Post.

Unit 4: Processing Invoices & Credit Notes

4.1 Data Collection

Invoices should be collated on a periodic basis and batched together with a batch header.

The batch header will help the auditors and is also a check for you. The batch total should equal the total on the screen after posting the invoices. Purchases and Sales batch totals are listed on pages 146 and 148.

If there are a lot of invoices they must be processed in batches of not more than 12.

Purchase invoices must also be separate from sales invoices.

DATA PROCESSING

Before entering Invoices or Credit Notes it is recommended that a Batch Control Slip is prepared. This is simply a list of the documents to be processed and can take the format of the sample Batch Control Slip printed below.

SALES INV.	SALES CREDIT	PURCHASE INV.	PURCHASE CREDIT

Tick as appropriate

PREPARED BY: _____

NOM. CODE	DATE	DETAILS	NET	TAX	GROSS

4.2 Purchase Invoices

The invoices required to complete Unit 4.2 are shown on pages 15–16.

To enter PURCHASE INVOICES:

> Choose PURCHASE LEDGER from the Main Menu
> Choose BATCHED DATA ENTRY
> Choose PURCHASE INVOICES from the Sub-Menu

The screen will display a clean "Input Sheet" and you will be required to enter the details of each invoice onto this "form". Normally – but not always – you will complete one line for each invoice.

Enter the Account Reference in the A/C column. If you cannot remember the reference press the F4 key and a list of accounts will be displayed or refer to your Purchase Accounts list. Use the Up and Down arrow keys to move over the appropriate name and press ENTER.

The full Account name will immediately be displayed at the top of the screen, and the cursor will move onto the Date column.

The Date should be entered as a six figure number where the first two numbers represent the day of the month, the next two figures represent the month number and the last two digits represent the year. eg 090891 is the 9th August 1991.

If the date on the invoice coincides with the 'system' date, ie the date you entered before the Main Menu appeared at the beginning of the session, you can press F5 Function Key and the system will automatically enter the system date for you. If the date does not coincide with the system date, you just type it in.

The cursor will then move onto the Inv. column. In this column you can enter up to six alphabetic or numerical characters as a reference for the invoice, (generally the invoice number).

The cursor will then move onto the N/C column (nominal code). Here you can enter a valid Nominal account code, and the name will be displayed at the top of the screen. Again if you cannot remember the N/C press F4 Function Key and a list will be displayed on the screen, or refer to your Nominal Code listing.

For Family Favourites the nominal account codes for Purchases are:

> 5000   Clothes
> 5001   Sportswear   (Ignore the Department code by pressing ENTER)
> 5002   Household

The cursor will then move onto the Details column. Here you can enter up to 19 characters briefly to describe the invoice details.

The cursor will then move onto the Net column. You should enter the Net amount shown on the invoice in this column. There are two exceptions.

i) You are splitting the invoice across more than one nominal account, in which case you should enter the Net amount for the appropriate normal code.

ii) You wish to enter the gross amount and allow the system to automatically calculate and deduct the appropriate amount of tax.

Nikey

75 London Road
Leicester

Invoice

To:
Family Favourites
Lichfield Rd Ind Est
Tamworth
Staffs

Customer Order Number:	Despatched by:	Invoice no:	Invoice Date / Tax Point:
FF 124		3485	01/1/94

Cat Number:	Quantity:	Description:	Price:	£	p
1108	25	Jog Pants	7.00	175	00
1109	15	Red Sweatshirt	8.50	127	50
0704	30	White Bikini	7.00	210	00
1105	30	Sweatshirts	4.50	135	00
1001	15	Hang Ten Jacket	15.00	225	00
1002	15	Long John wet suit	20.00	300	00

			£	p
		Gross Value of Goods	1172	50
		Less Discount		
		Net Value of Goods		
Code 5001		Plus V.A.T. @ 17.5%	205	19
E & O E		Invoice total	1377	69

Terms: V.A.T. Registration No:

BETTERWARES

7 Sutton Way, Sutton Coldfield, West Midlands.

Invoice

To:
Family Favourites
Lichfield Rd Ind Est
Tamworth
Staffs

Customer Order Number:	Despatched by:	Invoice No:	Invoice Date / Tax Point:
FF122	British Rail	2347	04/01/94

Cat Number:	Quantity:	Description:	Price:	£	p
5403	20	18 pc tea set	9.25	185	00
5201	3	50 pc household set	25.30	75	90
5401	9	30 pc everymeal set	9.30	83	70
5402	20	12 pc tea set	6.75	135	00
5605	7	Compact oven	43.25	302	75
5607	3	Jug Kettle	13.25	39	75
5606	12	Toaster	13.25	159	00

			£	p
		Gross Value of Goods	981	00
		Less Discount		
		Net Value of Goods		
		Plus V.A.T. @ 17.5%	171	68
E & O E		Invoice total	1152	68

Terms: V.A.T. Registration No.:

Racquets & Balls

26 New Invention,
Walsall.

Invoice

To:
Family Favourites
Lichfield Rd Ind Est
Tamworth
Staffs

Customer Order Number:	Despatched by:	Invoice no:	Invoice Date / Tax Point:
FF 120	Van	Pt 224	9/1/94

Cat Number:	Quantity:	Description:	Price:	£	p
1107	15	Grey sweatshirt	5.50	82	50
1110	35	Blue Polo Shirt	5.00	175	00
1106	10	Shorts	4.50	45	00
1401	30	Pilot fitness shoes	12.50	375	00
1402	25	Continental fitness shoes	18.50	462	50
1403	25	Jack running shoe	14.00	350	00
1404	25	Sydney running shoe	13.00	325	00

			£	p
		Gross Value of Goods	1815	00
		Less Discount		
		Net Value of Goods		
		Plus V.A.T. @ 17.5%	317	63
E & O E		Invoice total	2132	63

Terms: V.A.T. Registration No:

Mann Richards

Unit 4, Brigetown Ind. Est. Bridgetown. Walsall.

Invoice

To:
Family Favourites
Lichfield Rd Ind Es:
Tamworth
Staffs

Customer Order Number:	Despatched by:	Invoice No:	Invoice Date / Tax Point:
FF 123		1011	7/1/94

Cat Number:	Quantity:	Description:	Price:	£	p
4908	9	Goblin Cleaner	36.75	330	75
5601	9	Kenwood Chef	66.00	594	00
4906	3	Steam Iron	14.60	43	80
5604	2	Food Processor	50.00	100	00
5602	12	Liquidiser attachment	10.00	120	00

			£	p
		Gross Value of Goods	1188	55
		Less Discount		
		Net Value of Goods		
		Plus V.A.T. @ 17.5%	208	00
E & O E		Invoice total	1396	55

Terms: V.A.T. Registration No.:

15

Levis

3 Broad Street,
Birmingham.

Invoice

To : Family Favourites
Lichfield Rd Ind Est
Tamworth
Staffs

Customer Order Number :	Despatched by :	Invoice no :	Invoice Date / Tax Point :
FF 125	Carrier	P1234	2/1/94

Cat Number :	Quantity :	Description :	Price :	£	p
0504	40	Sweatshirt	4.54	181	60
0201	30	2 pce. suit	9.10	273	00

		£	p
	Gross Value of Goods	454	60
	Less Discount		
	Net Value of Goods		
	Plus V.A.T. @ 17.5%	79	56
E & O E	Invoice total	534	16

Terms :   V.A.T. Registration No :

Britannia

Unit 4, Green Lane, Cannock.

Invoice

To : Family Favourites
Lichfield Rd Ind Est
Tamworth
Staffs

Customer Order Number :	Despatched by :	Invoice no :	Invoice Date / Tax Point :
FF 121		7510	5/1/94

Cat Number :	Quantity :	Description :	Price :	£	p
0203	60	Beach Dress	4.54	272	40
0505	24	3 pc suit - & skirts	13.63	327	12
0202	10	Embroidered sundress	5.90	59	00
0402	15	Pleat front trousers	5.90	88	50

		£	p
	Gross Value of Goods	747	02
	Less Discount		
	Net Value of Goods		
	Plus V.A.T. @ 17.5%	130	73
E & O E	Invoice total	877	75

Terms :   V.A.T. Registration No :

The cursor will then move onto the Tc column (tax code). At present we have established four tax rates, namely:

    T0 Zero rated items
    T1 Standard (17.5%) rated items
    T2 Exempt items
    T9 Transactions not subject to Tax

When you have entered the tax code, the appropriate tax rate will be displayed at the top of the screen, and the VAT amount will be calculated.

Function Key F9 will automatically enter tax code T1. It is possible to get the system to automatically calculate the tax amount either by:

i)   Enter > and the system will add tax to the figure in the Net column, or

ii) Enter < and the system will deduct tax from the figure in the Net column and display the changed nett value as well as the tax value.

On occasions when you want to post items from one invoice to more than one Nominal account, complete a separate line for each nominal account.

You can complete 12 invoices on one screen.

Note: you can save time by using Function Key F6 to replicate the details from the previous line.

CORRECTING INVOICE DETAILS

If you notice that you have made a mistake on a previous entry you can move the cursor back to enter the correct value by using the four arrow keys on the numerical pad, and then type over the details.

RECORDING INVOICE DETAILS

Up to now you have simply entered the invoice details onto the screen; they have not been recorded on the ledger files.

When you have completed the 'Input sheet' you should press ESC.

The system will then ask:

> *Do you want to:*   *Post*   *Edit*   *Abandon*

Check with your batch total. If all the details on the screen are correct, answer 'Post' by pressing ENTER over the Post command.

The system will then update the ledgers with the invoice details on the screen. The 'Input Screen' will then be cleared and you can continue to enter more invoice details.

However, if you have to make some corrections, (ie the total on the screen does not equal your batch total) answer 'Edit'.

Again move to the incorrect details using the arrow keys. If you have no more invoices to enter, press ESC when you have a clean 'Input' screen and the system will return to the appropriate menu, otherwise carry on entering the details of any remaining invoices.

UPDATING LEDGERS

When you 'post' the details entered on screen the system will display message:

Updating audit trail.

The processes that are now taking place for each invoice are as follows:

i)   The details are entered onto the next available space on the Audit Trail.

ii)   The outstanding balance on either the Sales account or Purchase Account is then increased by the GROSS amount.

iii) The nominal ledger accounts are then updated as follows:

Purchase invoice

Credit 'Creditor's Control' by gross invoice value
Debit 'Nominal Account' by net invoice value
Debit 'Tax Control' by Tax amount

Sales invoice

Debit 'Debtor's control' by gross invoice value
Credit 'Nominal Account' by net invoice value
Credit 'Tax control' by Tax amount

The processing of sales invoices will be very similar and so this section should be used for reference.

4.3 Sales Invoices

The invoices required to complete section 4.3 are shown on pages 19–21.

To enter SALES INVOICES:

Choose SALES LEDGER from the Main Menu
Choose BATCHED DATA ENTRY
Choose SALES INVOICES from the Sub-Menu

Adopt the same practice as purchases except enter the Sales Nominal Ledger Codes:

4000   Clothes
4001   Sportswear
4002   Household

Enter the Net Value of Goods.

Please refer to Unit 4.2 if you are unsure of the procedure.

4.4 Credit notes

The entry of credit note details (see page 23) operates in exactly the same way as the invoice entry routine. Please refer to Unit 4.2 if you are unsure of the procedure.

As with invoices, all credit notes issued to accounts should be collected, batched and coded appropriately.

FAMILY FAVOURITES

Lichfield Road Industrial Estate, TAMWORTH

Invoice

To: Mrs J Whitby
Homeleigh
Tamworth Rd
Amington
Tamworth, Staffs

Customer Order Number :	Despatched by :	Invoice No :	Invoice Date / Tax Point :
Phone	Van	7001	3/1/94

Cat Number :	Quantity :	Description :	Price :	£	p
4908	5	Goblin Cleaner	54.99	274	95
5403	5	18 pc Tea Set	13.99	69	95
5601	2	Kenwood Chef	99.99	199	98
		Gross Value of Goods		544	88
		Less Discount		54	49
		Net Value of Goods		490	39
		Plus V.A.T. @ 17.5%		85	82
E & O E		Invoice total		576	21

Terms :   V.A.T. Registration No. : 84362957

FAMILY FAVOURITES

Lichfield Road Industrial Estate, TAMWORTH

Invoice

To: Mrs T Blankley
5 Ingold Ave
Walsall
West Midlands

Customer Order Number :	Despatched by :	Invoice No :	Invoice Date / Tax Point :
12352	Van	7002	5/1/94

Cat Number :	Quantity :	Description :	Price :	£	p
0704	12	White Bikini	13.99	167	88
0504	10	Sweatshirt	9.99	99	90
0203	10	Beach Dress	9.99	99	90
		Gross Value of Goods		367	68
		Less Discount		36	77
		Net Value of Goods		330	91
		Plus V.A.T. @ 17.5%		57	91
E & O E		Invoice total		388	82

Terms :   V.A.T. Registration No. : 84362957

FAMILY FAVOURITES

Lichfield Road Industrial Estate, TAMWORTH

Invoice

To: Mr A Holloway
The Fairings
Four Oaks
West Midlands

Customer Order Number :	Despatched by :	Invoice No :	Invoice Date / Tax Point :
Phone 6/1/92	Van	7003	7/1/94

Cat Number :	Quantity :	Description :	Price :	£	p
1105	75	Sweatshirts	14.99	374	75
1106	12	Adida Shorts	8.99	107	88
1001	10	Hang Ten Jacket	29.99	299	90
1002	10	Long Johns	39.99	399	90
1108	10	Jog Pants	13.99	139	90
		Gross Value of Goods		1322	33
		Less Discount		132	23
		Net Value of Goods		1190	10
		Plus V.A.T. @ 17.5%		208	27
E & O E		Invoice total		1398	37

Terms :   V.A.T. Registration No. : 84362957

FAMILY FAVOURITES

Lichfield Road Industrial Estate, TAMWORTH

Invoice

To: Mrs J Williams
3 The Avenue
Polesworth
Tamworth
Staffs

Customer Order Number :	Despatched by :	Invoice No :	Invoice Date / Tax Point :
Phone cc	Van	7004	9/1/94

Cat Number :	Quantity :	Description :	Price :	£	p
0201	6	Three piece suit casual 2 white, lemon, coral	19.99	119	94
0505	4	Three piece 'office' suit: 2 skirts	29.99	119	96
0504	10	Brushed cotton sweatshirt	9.99	99	90
		Gross Value of Goods		339	80
		Less Discount		33	98
		Net Value of Goods		305	82
		Plus V.A.T. @ 17.5%		53	52
E & O E		Invoice total		359	34

Terms :   V.A.T. Registration No. : 84362957

FAMILY FAVOURITES

Lichfield Road Industrial Estate, TAMWORTH

Invoice

To: Mrs H Whitehouse
26 Thorne Rd
Sutton Coldfield
West Midlands

Customer Order Number :	Despatched by :	Invoice No :	Invoice Date / Tax Point :
1637B	Van	7005	13/1/94

Cat Number :	Quantity :	Description :	Price :	£	p
0201	30	3 Pc Suits (6 each size)	19.99	599	70
0203	25	Beach Dress (5 each size)	9.99	249	75

	£	p
Gross Value of Goods	849	45
Less Discount	84	95
Net Value of Goods	764	50
Plus V.A.T. @ 17.5%	133	79
Invoice total	898	29

E & O E

Terms :   V.A.T. Registration No. : 84362957

FAMILY FAVOURITES

Lichfield Road Industrial Estate, TAMWORTH

Invoice

To: Mrs C Evans
42 Oak View
Rugeley
Staffs

Customer Order Number :	Despatched by :	Invoice No :	Invoice Date / Tax Point :
Phone	Rail	7007	22/1/94

Cat Number :	Quantity :	Description :	Price :	£	p
5401	10	30 pc Dinner Set	13.99	139	90
5402	20	12 pc Tea Set	9.99	199	80
5403	10	18 pc Tea Set	13.99	139	90
5601	2	Kenwood Chef	99.99	199	98
5605	3	Kenwood Oven	64.99	194	97
5607	2	Kenwood Jug Kettle	19.99	39	98

	£	p
Gross Value of Goods	914	53
Less Discount	91	45
Net Value of Goods	823	08
Plus V.A.T. @ 17.5%	144	04
Invoice total	967	12

E & O E

Terms :   V.A.T. Registration No. : 84362957

FAMILY FAVOURITES

Lichfield Road Industrial Estate, TAMWORTH

Invoice

To: Mrs A Nolan
14 Hatherton St
Cheslyn Hay
West Midlands

Customer Order Number :	Despatched by :	Invoice No :	Invoice Date / Tax Point :
190B	Rail	7006	19/1/94

Cat Number :	Quantity :	Description :	Price :	£	p
0202	20	Embroidered cotton dress	12.99	259	80
0203	15	Beach Dress	9.99	149	85
0504	15	Brushed cotton Sweatshirt	9.99	149	85

	£	p
Gross Value of Goods	559	50
Less Discount	55	95
Net Value of Goods	503	55
Plus V.A.T. @ 17.5%	88	12
Invoice total	591	67

E & O E

Terms :   V.A.T. Registration No. : 84362957

FAMILY FAVOURITES

Lichfield Road Industrial Estate, TAMWORTH

Invoice

To: Mrs M Harris
Sevenoaks
Long Lane
Lichfield
Staffs

Customer Order Number :	Despatched by :	Invoice No :	Invoice Date / Tax Point :
904C	Van	7008	24/1/94

Cat Number :	Quantity :	Description :	Price :	£	p
1107	5	Grey Sweatshirts	10.99	54	95
1109	10	Red Sweatshirts	17.99	179	90
1110	5	Blue Polo Shirts	9.99	49	95

	£	p
Gross Value of Goods	284	80
Less Discount	28	48
Net Value of Goods	256	32
Plus V.A.T. @ 17.5%	44	86
Invoice total	301	18

E & O E

Terms :   V.A.T. Registration No. : 84362957

FAMILY FAVOURITES

Lichfield Road Industrial Estate, TAMWORTH

Invoice

To : Mr P Weir
32 Cedar Rd
Cannock
Staffs

Customer Order Number :	Despatched by :	Invoice No :	Invoice Date / Tax Point :
904D	Rail	7010	31/1/94

Cat Number :	Quantity :	Description :	Price :	£	p
1401	20	Pilot Fitness Shoes	24.99	499	80
1402	20	Continental Fitness Shoes	36.99	739	80
1403	20	Jack Running Shoes	27.99	559	80
1404	20	Sydney Running Shoes	25.99	519	80
		(4 each size) 6. 7. 8. 9. 10			

	Gross Value of Goods			2319	20
	Less Discount			231	92
	Net Value of Goods			2087	28
	Plus V.A.T. @ 17.5%			365	27
E & O E	Invoice total			2452	55

Terms :   V.A.T. Registration No. : 84362957

FAMILY FAVOURITES

Lichfield Road Industrial Estate, TAMWORTH

Invoice

To : Miss J Goldingay
71 Chiltern Rd
Wolverhampton
West Midlands

Customer Order Number :	Despatched by :	Invoice No :	Invoice Date / Tax Point :
Phone 20/1/92	Van	7009	31/1/94

Cat Number :	Quantity :	Description :	Price :	£	p
5601	10	Kenwood Chef	99.99	999	90
5602	10	Liquidiser Attach.	15.99	159	90
5606	10	Kenwood Toaster	19.99	199	90
5605	5	Kenwood Grill	64.99	649	90

	Gross Value of Goods			2009	60
	Less Discount			200	96
	Net Value of Goods			1808	64
	Plus V.A.T. @ 17.5%			316	51
E & O E	Invoice total			2125	15

Terms :   V.A.T. Registration No. : 84362957

SALES CREDIT NOTES

To enter SALES CREDIT NOTES:

> Choose SALES LEDGER from the Main Menu
> Choose BATCHED DATA ENTRY
> Choose SALES CREDIT NOTES from the Sub-Menu

PURCHASE CREDIT NOTES

To enter PURCHASE CREDIT NOTES:

> Choose PURCHASE LEDGER from the Main Menu
> Choose BATCHED DATA ENTRY
> Choose PURCHASE CREDIT NOTES from the Sub-Menu

When you have finished the entries press the ESC key and the system will post the details to the ledgers.

4.5 Matching Credit Notes against Invoices

After credit notes have been posted they then have to be 'matched' against the invoice to which they relate, or against the oldest balance.

> Choose SALES LEDGER from the Main menu
> Choose SALES RECEIPTS from the Sub-Menu

The Bank nominal Ledger Accounts Code 1200 will be flashing; press ENTER

> A/C Ref, this is the customers reference; enter the customer reference WEIR.
> Enter the date of the credit note
> Type CREDIT against the cheque number and press ENTER for amount
> Move the cursor onto Manual using the right arrow key
> Move the highlighted bar over the credit note, using the down arrow key, and then press ENTER.

You will be prompted to select: Full   Part   Discount   Cancel

> Select 'Full' by pressing ENTER

You should notice that the value of the credit note is reduced to zero and the word Full appears on the left side of the screen against the credit note, whilst the cheque balance at the top of the screen is now the value of the credit note.

Now using the Up arrow key, move up over the invoice to which the credit note relates and press ENTER. Again you will be prompted Full Part Discount Cancel. As you want part, press ENTER over Part. The prompt will ask you to enter the amount to part pay. Enter the appropriate figure and press ENTER.

The invoice is now marked as partly paid, and shows the reduced amount outstanding, now press ESC and Post.

The same procedure is carried out for credit notes in the Purchase Ledger.

Note that although you used Sales Receipts/Purchase Payments, no money actually went into or out of the bank, it was merely a way to match the credit note against the invoice.

FAMILY FAVOURITES

Lichfield Road Industrial Estate, TAMWORTH

Mr P Weir	31/1/94
32 Cedar Road	
Cannock	
Staffs	1234

| Reason for Credit | Quantity and Description | Total credit (Excluding V.A.T.) | V.A.T. Credited | |
			Rate	Amount
Split Sole	1403 a pair running shoes	27.99		
	-discount	2.80		
		25.19	17.5%	4.41
				29.60

Credit Note

FAMILY FAVOURITES

Lichfield Road Industrial Estate, TAMWORTH

Mrs J Whitby	5/1/94
Homeleigh	
Tamworth Rd	
Amington	1235

| Reason for Credit | Quantity and Description | Total credit (Excluding V.A.T.) | V.A.T. Credited | |
			Rate	Amount
Broken Cup	5403 1-18 piece tea set	13.99		
	-discount	1.40		
		12.59	17.5%	2.20
				14.79

Credit Note

Racquets & Balls

26 New invention, Walsall.

Family Favourites		VAT Reg. No.	
Lichfield Rd Ind Est			
Tamworth	No. 1/16	Date : 16.01.94	
Staffs			

| Reason for Credit | Quantity and Description | Total credit (Excluding V.A.T.) | V.A.T. Credited | |
			Rate	Amount
Split Sole	1 pair Jack running shoes 1403	14.00	17.5%	2.45
				16.45

Credit Note

BETTERWARES

7 Sutton Way, Sutton Coldfield, West Midlands.

Credit Note

Family Favourites		VAT Reg. No.	
Lichfield Rd Ind Est			
Tamworth	No. 01/12	Date : 12.1.94	
Staffs			

| Reason for Credit | Quantity and Description | Total credit (Excluding V.A.T.) | V.A.T. Credited | |
			Rate	Amount
Broken cup	1 - 18 pce tea set 5403	9.25	17.5%	1.62
				10.87

Credit Note

Unit 5: Processing Cheques Received and Paid

The program allows payments to be allocated wholly or partially to individual outstanding invoices.

The method for entering payment is to call up each account in turn, enter the payment details (date, ref. and cheque amount) and then select whether you wish to enter them manually.

Either way you should end up with a screen showing the allocated transactions and a cheque balance of zero.

5.1 Cheques received from customers

To enter sales receipts (page 25):

> Choose SALES LEDGER from the Main Menu
> Choose SALES RECEIPTS from the Sub-Menu

The system will ask for A/C Ref.

Enter the appropriate account reference and the corresponding name will be displayed alongside.

Continue by entering the date, cheque number and cheque amount alongside the relevant prompts.

When you have entered these details the system will now display all outstanding transactions for this Account and ask:

> *Method of payment?*   *Automatic*   *Manual*

The cursor will be positioned over the word Automatic.

AUTOMATIC ALLOCATION

If you select automatic allocation, the computer will start with the first transaction on the screen and mark this as being fully paid, providing sufficient money is on the cheque. It will then reduce the cheque balance accordingly, move to the next invoice and repeat the same procedure until the cheque balance is zero.

MANUAL ALLOCATION

If you select manual allocation, then you use the Up and Down arrow keys to select which of the invoices are to be paid, either fully or partially. This routine will be used to allocate settlement discount.

Move the cursor using the arrow keys over the transaction that you want to pay and press ENTER.

The system will now ask:

> *Type of Payment?*   *Full*   *Part*   *Discount*   *Cancel*

Make the appropriate selection.

When you are satisfied with all the allocations that you have made, press ESC and Post.

CHEQUES RECEIVED FROM CUSTOMERS

SPECIMEN   31/12   19**93**   56-81-34
National Westminster Bank PLC
St. Clair Branch
16 The Square, St. Clair, Norfolk
Pay *Family Favourites Ltd* or order
Eightysix pounds 50p £86 — 50
H. Whitehouse
WHITEHOUSE
⑈326071⑈ 56⑈ 8139: 00925817⑈

16-99-83
Williams & Glyn's Bank plc
Trent branch
17 High Street Trent Surrey AB1 2CD
PAY *FAMILY FAVOURITES* OR ORDER
ONE HUNDRED & THIRTYFOUR POUNDS 70p £134 — 70
DATE 10/1 19**94**
T. Blankley ⑈235532⑈ 18⑈ 99831: 19832922⑈ T. BLANKLEY

SPECIMEN
Williams & Glyn's Bank p
Trent branch
17 High Street Trent Surrey AB1 2CD
PAY *Family Favourites* OR ORDER
Forty pounds only £40 — 00
DATE 1/1 19**94**
Mrs A NOLAN A. NOLAN
⑈235532⑈ 18⑈ 99831: 19832922⑈

Lloyds Bank   SPECIMEN 5/1 19**94** 30-20-00
PRIORY ROAD, NORWICH, NR1 9XX
Pay *FAMILY FAVOURITES* or order
SIXTY POUNDS & ELEVEN £60 — 11
NEW PENCE
Mrs M. Harris
⑈536125⑈ 30⑈ 2000: 0132398⑈ M. HARRIS

Midland Bank plc SPECIMEN 6/1 19**94** 40-51-20
21 North Street
Linton Bridge North Yorkshire
Pay *Family Favourites* or order
Seventythree pounds 63p £73 — 63
C Evans
⑈579059⑈ 90⑈ 5120: 00893912⑈ C. EVANS.

25

5.2 Cheques paid to Suppliers

To enter purchase payments (below):

Choose PURCHASE LEDGER POSTINGS from the Main Menu
Choose PURCHASE PAYMENTS from the Sub-Menu

Follow the same procedure as in Unit 5.1.

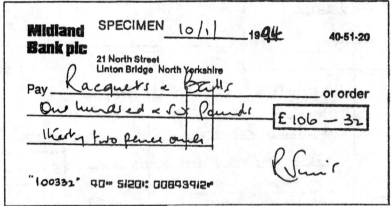

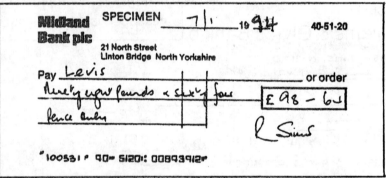

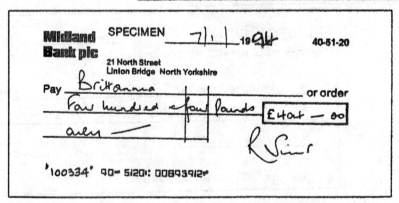

Unit 6: Setting Up a Petty Cash System

6.1 Cash Payments

The Manager has decided to introduce a Petty Cash System to cater for the small office cash items and general expenses.

To do this he raised a cheque for £200 on 1st January 1994, No. 100330, made out to Cash Code 1230. Each payment during the month (as listed on pages 28–29) must be supported by a Petty Cash Voucher and the total amount spent re-input at the beginning of the following month.

> Choose NOMINAL LEDGER from the Main Menu
> Choose JOURNAL ENTRIES from the Sub-Menu.

Enter Jnl ref Petty Cash (P/C1)

Date 01/01/94

CODE	DETAIL		Dr	Cr
1230	Petty Cash Cheque	T9	£200.00	
1200	Petty Cash Cheque			£200.00

When you have completed this, press ESC and Post.

Now go to PETTY CASH TRANSACTIONS and enter Petty Cash Vouchers

> Choose CASH PAYMENTS from the Sub-Menu.

Enter Petty Cash Voucher Nos. 1–12. You can use the Reference Column for Voucher Number (Folio).

To automatically calculate the VAT refer to Unit 4.2. Only do this where a VAT number is quoted.

A new account will have to be opened for Sundry Expenses 8206.

Remember to go to ACCOUNTS STRUCTURE to set up this new account. Enter the Yearly Budget as £240.

A print-out of the petty cash items can be obtained as follows.:

> Choose DAY BOOKS from the Nominal Ledger Structure
> Choose CASH PAYMENTS and [P]

6.2 Cash Receipts

The Petty Cash System will also allow the company to accept CASH for Cash and Carry items. The two cash sale Invoices (page 29) were paid for with cash which would be added to the Petty Cash Float. Enter these by:-

> Choose PETTY CASH TRANSACTIONS
> Choose CASH RECEIPTS from the Sub-Menu
> Enter Cash Sales Invoices 82 and 83

After completion of all the months cash transactions the Petty Cash balance can be checked by:

> Choose CONTROL ACCOUNTS
> Choose PETTY CASH
> Print out details to find the balance

Cash Payments

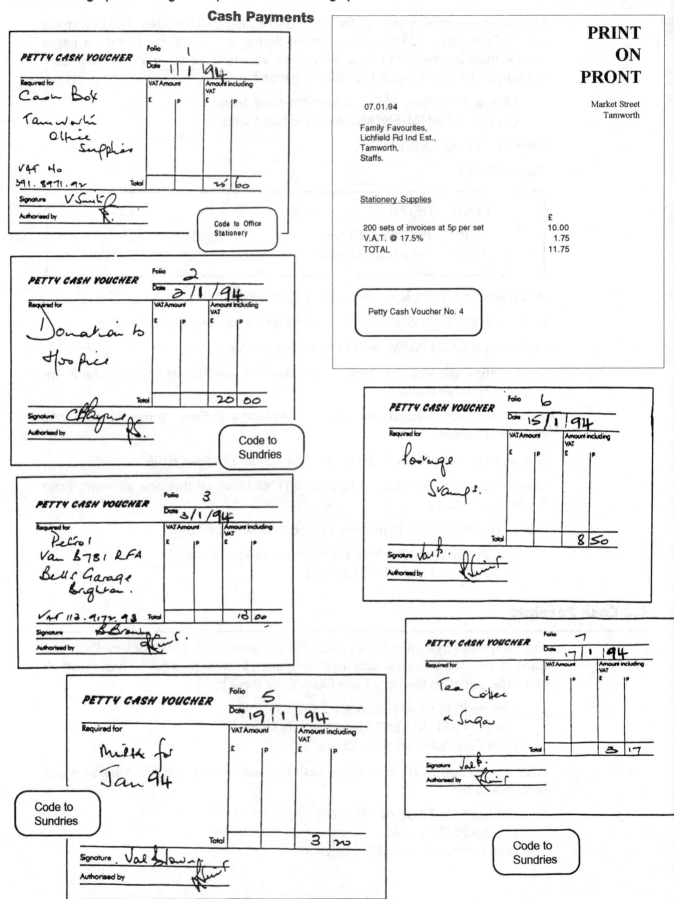

PETTY CASH VOUCHER

Folio 1
Date 1 / 1 / 94

Required for
Cash Box
Tamworth
Office
Supplies

VAT No
391. 8971. 92

Total — 25 60

Signature V Smith
Authorised by R.

Code to Office Stationery

PETTY CASH VOUCHER

Folio 2
Date 3 / 1 / 94

Required for
Donation to
Hospice

Total — 20 00

Signature C Reynolds
Authorised by R.

Code to Sundries

PETTY CASH VOUCHER

Folio 3
Date 3 / 1 / 94

Required for
Petrol
Van B781 RFA
Bells Garage
Brighton.

VAT 113. 9172. 93   Total — 13 00

Signature B Brown
Authorised by R.

PETTY CASH VOUCHER

Folio 5
Date 19 / 1 / 94

Required for
Milk for
Jan 94

Total — 3 20

Signature Val Brown
Authorised by

Code to Sundries

PRINT
ON
PRONT

Market Street
Tamworth

07.01.94

Family Favourites,
Lichfield Rd Ind Est.,
Tamworth,
Staffs.

Stationery Supplies

£
200 sets of invoices at 5p per set   10.00
V.A.T. @ 17.5%   1.75
TOTAL   11.75

Petty Cash Voucher No. 4

PETTY CASH VOUCHER

Folio 6
Date 15 / 1 / 94

Required for
Postage
Stamps.

Total — 8 50

Signature Val B.
Authorised by

PETTY CASH VOUCHER

Folio 7
Date 17 / 1 / 94

Required for
Tea Coffee
& Sugar

Total — 3 17

Signature Val B.
Authorised by

Code to Sundries

PETTY CASH VOUCHER

Folio 8
Date 21.1.94

Required for	VAT Amount £	p	Amount including VAT £	p
Petrol for Van B781 RFA Swanpvan Services				
VAT 123. 1672. 92	Total		15	00

Signature BBrown

Authorise

PETTY CASH VOUCHER

Folio 9
Date 24.1.94

Required for	VAT Amount £	p	Amount including VAT £	p
Window Cleaner				
	Total		23	00

Signature Val M

PETTY CASH VOUCHER

Folio 10
Date 25/1/94

Required for	VAT Amount £	p	Amount including VAT £	p
W H Smith Pens				
107. 007H. 91	Total		18	70

Signature Val Brown M

Authorised

PETTY CASH VOUCHER

Folio 11
Date 28/1/94

Required for	VAT Amount £	p	Amount including VAT £	p
Postages				
	Total		5	20

Signature Barnsley

PETTY CASH VOUCHER

Folio 12
Date 28/1/94

Required for	VAT Amount £	p	Amount including VAT £	p
Petrol for Van B781 RFA Bromford Services				
VAT No. 104. 9011. 91	Total		23	50

Signature BBrown

Authorised by

FAMILY FAVOURITES

Lichfield Road Industrial Estate, TAMWORTH

Sports for all
Atherstone
Warwicks

CASH SALE .82.   18/1/94

Ref	Description	Qty.	Unit Price		Total	
1110	Polo Shirt	20	9	99	199	80
1108	Jogging Pants	15	13	99	209	85
	Total				£409	65
	Plus VAT 17.5%				£71	69
					£481	34

FAMILY FAVOURITES

Lichfield Road Industrial Estate, TAMWORTH

Tamworth Fashions
2 George Street
Tamworth

CASH SALE .83.   28/1/94

Ref	Description	Qty.	Unit Price		Total	
0704	White Bikini	10	13	99	139	90
0505	Three Piece Suit	5	12	99	64	95
0203	Beach Dress	20	9	99	199	80
	Total				£404	65
	Plus VAT 17.5%				£70	81
					£475	46

This can be corrected through the Journal.

Again Choose JOURNAL ENTRIES and enter the following:

Jnl ref Petty Cash (P/C2)

Date 30/1/94

CODE	DETAIL		Dr	Cr
1200	Petty Cash Banked	T9		?
1230	Petty Cash Banked		?	

After Posting, check that the Petty Cash Balance has been adjusted to the required £200.

Unit 7: Processing Expenses

Other expenses which do not relate to the Sales or Purchase Ledger (shown on pages 31–33) will need to be paid by cheque or direct debit through the NOMINAL LEDGER. To do this:

Choose   NOMINAL LEDGER from the Main Menu
Choose   BANK TRANSACTIONS from the Sub-Menu
Press   ENTER and
select   BANK PAYMENTS and the required expense code.

NOTE: Some items will be subject to VAT and others will not (Select the appropriate T code). See Unit1.3 for an explanation of Tax Status.

Wages are paid direct to the bank, so post the TOTAL ONLY at this stage to the Wages Control Account.

The Standing Order is direct payment from the bank account, so instead of a cheque number enter S/O.

As previously shown, when you have completed these entries press the ESC key and the details will be automatically updated.

NOTE: The payment for the Inland Revenue clears Family Favourites tax liability and should be coded to 2210. It is the outstanding tax bill brought forward in the Trial Balance (see page 12).

It will be necessary to bring the Cash Book up to date by entering the Bank Charges (Code 7901). See over for details from Bank Statement.

There is also a Bank Giro Credit from Holloway which must be entered as an additional Sales Ledger Receipt.

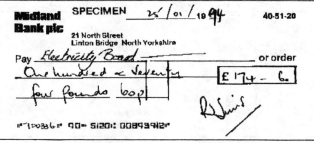

Birmingham Evening Herald

35 Broad Street, Birmingham.

Family Favourites,
Lichfield Rd Ind Est.,
Tamworth,
Staffs.

Date : 31.01.94

<u>Invoice for Advertising</u>

	£
Advertisments for the month of January 1992	132.13
V.A.T. @ 17.5%	23.12
TOTAL	155.25

ADAM FORD GARAGE

Upper Gungate, Tamworth.

Family Favourites,
Lichfield Rd Ind Est.,
Tamworth,
Staffs.

Date : 30.01.94

<u>Monthly Account for Petrol</u>

	£
137 gallons of 4 star petrol at £1.47 per gallon	197.11
V.A.T. @ 17.5%	34.49
TOTAL	231.60

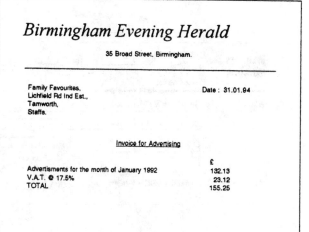

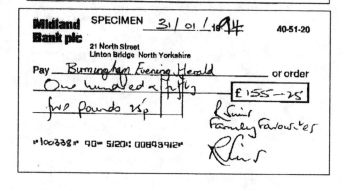

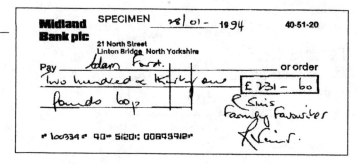

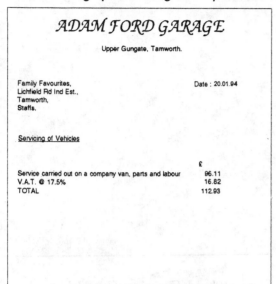

ADAM FORD GARAGE

Upper Gungate, Tamworth.

Family Favourites,   Date : 20.01.94
Lichfield Rd Ind Est.,
Tamworth,
Staffs.

<u>Servicing of Vehicles</u>

	£
Service carried out on a company van, parts and labour	96.11
V.A.T. @ 17.5%	16.82
TOTAL	112.93

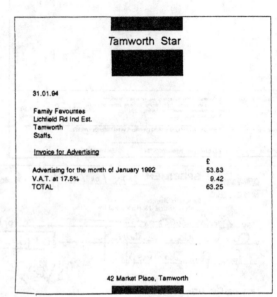

Tamworth Star

31.01.94

Family Favourites
Lichfield Rd Ind Est.
Tamworth
Staffs.

<u>Invoice for Advertising</u>

	£
Advertising for the month of January 1992	53.83
V.A.T. at 17.5%	9.42
TOTAL	63.25

42 Market Place, Tamworth

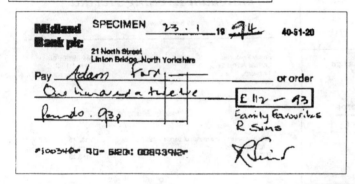

PRINT
ON
PRONT

Market Street
Tamworth

17.01.94

Family Favourites,
Lichfield Rd Ind Est.,
Tamworth,
Staffs.

<u>Stationery Supplies</u>

	£
200 sets of invoices at 5p per set	9.79
V.A.T. @ 17.5%	1.71
TOTAL	11.50

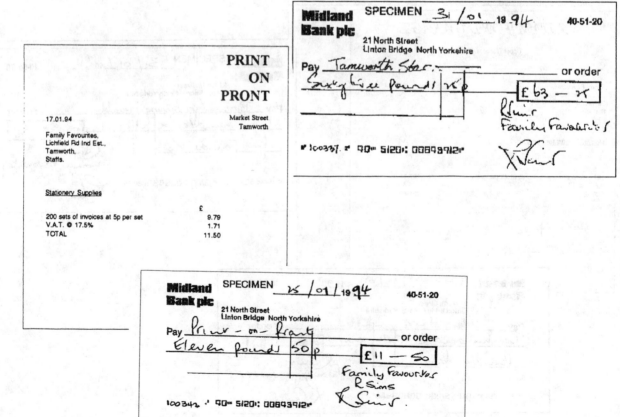

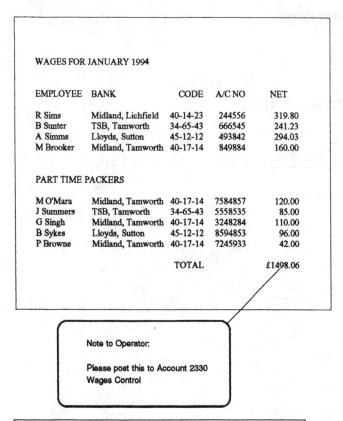

WAGES FOR JANUARY 1994

EMPLOYEE	BANK	CODE	A/C NO	NET
R Sims	Midland, Lichfield	40-14-23	244556	319.80
B Sunter	TSB, Tamworth	34-65-43	666545	241.23
A Simms	Lloyds, Sutton	45-12-12	493842	294.03
M Brooker	Midland, Tamworth	40-17-14	849884	160.00

PART TIME PACKERS

M O'Mara	Midland, Tamworth	40-17-14	7584857	120.00
J Summers	TSB, Tamworth	34-65-43	5558535	85.00
G Singh	Midland, Tamworth	40-17-14	3248284	110.00
B Sykes	Lloyds, Sutton	45-12-12	8594853	96.00
P Browne	Midland, Tamworth	40-17-14	7245933	42.00
			TOTAL	£1498.06

Note to Operator:

Please post this to Account 2330 Wages Control

Standing Order Mandate

To : Midland Bank Ltd.

Address : 21 North Street, Linton Bridge, North Yorkshire.

	Bank	Branch title (not address)	Code number
Please Pay	T.S.B.	Lichfield	30-08-27

	Beneficiary	Account Number
for the credit of	Grabber Properties	1 3 7 0 5 6 2

	Amount in figures	Amount in words
the sum of	479.17	

	Date and amount of 1st payment		Date and frequency
commencing	1/8/93	And thereafter every	4th of Month
	*now		

	Date and amount of last payment	
*until		Machine operator please note this is monthly rent, code 7100 Date 1/1/92

quoting the reference

* This instruction cancels any previous order in favour of the beneficiary named above, under this reference.

+ If the amount of the periodic payments vary they should be incorporated in a schedule overleaf.

Special instructions :

Signature : *R Sims* Date : 1/8/94

Title and number of account to be debited   Family Favourites Ltd   6 1 0 2 1 3 9 7

Note : The bank will not undertake to

(i) make any references to Value Added Tax or pay a stated sum "plus VAT"

(ii) advise payer's addresses to beneficiary

(iii) advise beneficiary of inability to pay

(iv) request beneficiary's banker to advise beneficiary of receipt

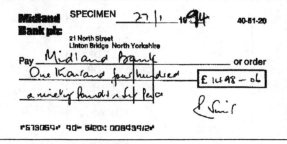

Midland Bank plc   SPECIMEN 27/1 1994   40-51-20

21 North Street
Linton Bridge North Yorkshire

Pay Midland Bank   or order

One thousand four hundred
and ninety pounds & six pence   £ 1498 - 06

R Sims

Midland Bank plc   SPECIMEN 19/1 1994   40-51-20

21 North Street
Linton Bridge North Yorkshire

Pay Inland Revenue   or order

Seventy five pounds
eighty nine pence   £75 - 89

R Sims

Please Note:

The payment for the Inland Revenue clears Family Favourites' tax liability and should be coded 2210 (see Unit 3.3).

It will be necessary to bring the Cash Book up to date by entering the Bank Charges (Code 7901). See over for details from Bank Statement.

Also there is a Bank Giro Credit from Holloway which must be entered as an additional Sales Ledger Receipt.

Statement of account with

Midland Bank plc	SPECIMEN <u>30 January</u> 19 <u>94</u>	40-51-20
	21 North Street Linton Bridge North Yorkshire	

Type of Account :	Name :	Account Number :
Current	Family Favourites	00893912

Date	Description	Withdrawals	Deposits	Balance	
1.01.94	BROUGHT FORWARD			1106.50	*
2.01.94	Credits		40.00	1146.50	*
3.01.94	100330	200.00		946.50	*
8.01.94	Standing order - Grabber Properties	479.17		467.33	*
8.01.94	Credits		133.74	601.07	*
11.01.94	100341	700.00		98.93DR	*
10.01.94	103331	98.64			
	103334	404.00		601.57DR	*
12.01.94	103332	106.32		707.89DR	*
12.01.94	103333	75.89		783.78DR	*
25.01.94	100340	112.93		896.71DR	*
28.01.94	100336	174.60		1071.31DR	*
20.01.94	100342	11.50		1082.81DR	*
31.01.94	Bank Charges	31.97		1114.78DR	*
31.01.94	Bank Giro Credit - A Holloway		98.62	1016.16DR	*

Note to Operator:

Enter bank charges and Giro credit into cash book.

Details of rates and calculation of any interest charged are available on request from your branch. Abbreviations: *Credit Balance DR Overdrawn Balance S Sub Total (Intermediate Balance)

Unit 8: Journal Entries

The company needs to charge the gross wages and the employers contribution in total, and collect the Tax and National Insurance for later payment to the INLAND REVENUE. This is done by crediting these deductions from the wages to special Control Accounts which then show the amounts owed to the Inland Revenue.

To allocate the wages to the correct accounts it is necessary to make the following journal entries.

8.1 Wages

Choose NOMINAL LEDGER from the Main Menu
Choose JOURNALS from the Sub-Menu

Enter the date (30/1/94) and the reference (JNL.2)

JOURNAL ENTRIES		Dr	Cr
Code 7003	Description JAN Wages	1653.00	
Code 7006	Description JAN Wages	52.00	
Code 2210	Description JAN Wages		102.94
Code 2211	Description JAN Wages		104.00
Code 2330	Description JAN Wages		1498.06
		1705.00	1705.00

The totals should then equal NIL.

Press ESC and Post.

8.2 Trial Balance

Now take out a TRIAL BALANCE

Choose TRIAL BALANCE from the Sub-Menu.

Enter (P) to Print.

Nominal Ledger Reports – Trial Balance

Ref	Accounts name	Debit	Credit
0011	Leasehold Property	10000.00	
0050	Motor Vehicles	5000.00	
1100	Debtors Control Account	10296.14	
1200	Bank Current Account		2043.44
1230	Petty Cash	200.00	
2100	Creditors Control Account		11742.70
2200	Tax Control Account		628.42
2210	P.A.Y.E.		102.94
2211	National Insurance		104.00
3000	Ordinary Shares		10000.00
3200	Profit And Loss Account		5303.36
4000	Sales Clothes		2309.43
4001	Sales Sportswear		3918.16
4002	Sales Household		3109.52
4950	Opening Stock Clothes	1287.10	
4951	Opening Stock Sportswear	1696.50	
4952	Opening Stock Household	738.50	
5000	Purchases Clothes	1201.62	
5001	Purchases Sportswear	2973.50	
5002	Purchases Household	2160.30	
7003	Staff Salaries	1653.00	
7006	Employers N.I.	52.00	
7100	Rent	479.17	
7200	Electricity	148.60	
7300	Fuel and Oil	240.94	
7301	Repairs and Servicing	96.11	
7501	Postage and Carriage	13.70	
7504	Office Stationery	57.49	
7801	Cleaning	23.00	
7901	Bank Charges	31.97	
8200	Advertising	185.96	
8204	Insurance	700.00	
8206	Sundry Expenses	26.37	
		39261.97	39261.97

Unit 9: Adjustments for Stock

9.1 Closing Stock

At the 31/1/94 a stock check was carried out and the value of the closing stock is as given below.

To show the true cost of sales for the period it is necessary, at this stage, to open an account in the Balance Sheet for closing stock. Three new Nominal Accounts will need to be created to cater for this:

Choose NOMINAL ACCOUNTS STRUCTURE
Choose ACCOUNT NAMES

and overtype the following:

1001   STOCK CLOTHES
1002   STOCK SPORTSWEAR
1003   STOCK HOUSEHOLD

Now to enter the journal:

Choose Nominal ledger Postings from the Main Menu
Choose JOURNAL ENTRIES from the Sub-Menu

Enter the date and the reference (i.e. JNL 3)

The closing stock in the Balance Sheet needs to be debited and the closing stock in the Profit and Loss Account needs to be credited.

The journal entry should read as follows:

CODE	DETAIL	ACCOUNT	DR	CR
1001	Closing Stock BS	Clothes	1362.62	
1002	Closing Stock BS	Sportswear	2309.00	
1003	Closing Stock BS	Household	2345.00	
5200	Closing Stock PL	Clothes		1362.62
5201	Closing Stock PL	Sportswear		2309.00
5202	Closing Stock PL	Household		2345.00

When you have completed this, press ESC and Post.

Unit 10: Adjustments for Accruals and Prepayments

In order to allocate the correct amount of expense to an accounting period, it is necessary to adjust the account at the end of each accounting period. This is done by adding to the expense to create a reserve, or reducing the expense with the value of a prepayment.

10.1 Accrued Expenses

As the company has not received the half yearly rates bill, provision for this must be made.

Choose NOMINAL LEDGER from the menu
Choose PREPAYMENTS and ACCRUALS
Choose ACCRUALS

Name	enter rates
N/C code	7103
Accrual N/C	2109
Value	£750
Month	3
Monthly	£250
Enter.	
Escape	[post]

10.2   Prepaid Expenses

The payments to Dornhill Insurance represents the total insurance for the year. Therefore a prepayment of eleven twelfths of seven hundred pounds needs to be adjusted.

Choose PREPAYMENTS and adopt the same procedure as accruals in 10.1

Insurance N/C	8204
Prepayments N/C	1103
Value	£700
Month	12
Monthly	£58.33
Enter.	
Escape	[post]

10.3 Adjustments Month End

In order to enter the Month End Adjustments you need to update the individual Nominal Accounts for the Profit & Loss Account and the Balance Sheet.

To do this:

Choose UTILITIES from the Main Menu
Choose MONTH END from the Sub-Menu
Choose PREPAYMENTS & ACCRUALS

An explanation of this activity will appear on the screen.

Press Return and [P] and Enter and print out the update for the Audit Trail.

Unit 11: Depreciation

This is an accounting technique for providing for the ageing and use of FIXED ASSETS. Family Favourites proprietor, Mr Sims, has decided to write off the £10,000 lease over its remaining 10 years life. To do this you will need to set up a new account for Depreciation of Lease No. 0012 (refer to Unit 2)

Similarly the Motor Van is depreciated over its estimated normal life span of four years (i.e. 25% per annum) using the straight line method.

To enter these transactions into the monthly accounts it is necessary to make the following journal entries.

11.1 Depreciation

Choose NOMINAL LEDGER
Choose DEPRECIATION
Enter Leasehold Property.
N/C0012 TP(S) 10% £10,000
Enter Motor van
N/C0051 TP(S) 25% £5,000

TP refers to the Type of Depreciation which can be either:

(S) Straight Line or
(R) Reducing Balance

11.2 Month End Entries

Choose UTILITIES
Choose MONTH END
Choose DEPRECIATION

An explanation of the effect of these entries will appear on the screen. Press enter and return to the nominal ledger. A print out of this activity can be obtained by entering [P].

Ref.	Accounts name	Debit	Credit
0011	Leasehold Property	10000.00	
0012	Depreciation Lease		83.33
0050	Motor Vehicles	5000.00	
0051	M/V Depreciation		104.17
1001	Stock Clothes	1362.62	
1002	Stock Sportswear	2309.00	
1003	Stock Household	2345.00	
1100	Debtors Control Account	10296.14	
1103	Prepayments	641.67	
1200	Bank Current Account		2043.44
1230	Petty Cash	200.00	
2100	Creditors Control Account		11742.70
2109	Accruals		250.00
2200	Tax Control Account		628.42
2210	P.A.Y.E.		102.94
2211	National Insurance		104.00
3000	Ordinary Shares		10000.00
3200	Profit And Loss Account		5303.36
4000	Sales Clothes		2309.43
4001	Sales Sportswear		3918.16
4002	Sales Household		3109.52
4950	Opening Stock Clothes	1287.10	
4951	Opening Stock Sportswear	1696.50	
4952	Opening Stock Household	738.50	
5000	Purchases Clothes	1201.62	
5001	Purchases Sportswear	2973.50	
5002	Purchases Household	2160.30	
5200	Closing Stock Clothes		1362.62
5201	Closing Stock Sportswear		2309.00
5202	Closing Stock Household		2345.00
7003	Staff Salaries	1653.00	
7006	Employers N.I.	52.00	
7100	Rent	479.17	
7103	General Rates	250.00	
7200	Electricity	148.60	
7300	Fuel and Oil	240.94	
7301	Repairs and Servicing	96.11	
7501	Postage and Carriage	13.70	
7504	Office Stationery	57.49	
7801	Cleaning	23.00	
7901	Bank Charges	31.97	
8000	Depreciation	187.50	
8200	Advertising	185.96	
8204	Insurance	58.33	
8206	Sundry Expenses	26.37	
		45716.09	45716.09

Nominal Ledger Reports – Trial Balance

Unit 12: Production of Monthly Accounts

Through the entire data entry process the program has been maintaining and updating the Nominal Ledger and Trial Balance.

From the Trial Balance the system is now able to produce a Trading and Profit and Loss Account, provided you set up the required parameters.

But firstly you need to print out the updated TRIAL BALANCE from the Nominal Ledger. To do this:

Choose NOMINAL LEDGER from the Main Menu
Choose TRIAL BALANCE
Enter [P] for Print

12.1 Trading and profit and loss account

The Trading and Profit and Loss Account is subdivided into four sections:

SALES   PURCHASES   DIRECT EXPENSES   OVERHEADS

The program calculates the Gross Profit by subtracting the Purchases and Direct Expenses from the Sales. As Family Favourites is not a manufacturing company no direct expenses are included.

Net Profit is calculated by subtracting the Overheads from the Gross Profit. Before you can produce this report you must establish a LAYOUT OF ACCOUNTS within each section.

From the program select as follows:

Choose NOMINAL LEDGER from the Main Menu
Choose NOMINAL ACCOUNT STRUCTURE from the Sub-Menu
Choose PROFIT AND LOSS ACCOUNT
Then select SALES from the list

The following will appear on your screen.

Sales	Sterling	Date:	
Category Heading		Low	High
UNUSED CATEGORY			
UNUSED CATEGORY			
UNUSED CATEGORY			
UNUSED CATEGORY			
UNUSED CATEGORY			
UNUSED CATEGORY			
UNUSED CATEGORY			
UNUSED CATEGORY			

Type in the following under the category headings, low and high parameters, overtype where necessary:

Category Heading	Low	High
Sales Clothes	4000	4000
Sales Sportswear	4001	4001
Sales Household	4002	4002

On completion, press ESC to return to the previous screen.

Select Purchases from the list and enter the following:

Opening Stock Clothes	4950	4950
Opening Stock Sportswear	4951	4951
Opening Stock Household	4952	4952
Purchases Clothes	5000	5000
Purchases Sportswear	5001	5001
Purchases Household	5002	5002
Closing Stock Clothes	5200	5200
Closing Stock Sportswear	5201	5201
Closing Stock Household	5202	5202

On completion, press ESC and return to the previous screen.

We have no Direct Expenses, so move onto Overheads.

The following are Overheads and you are required to enter them in exactly the same way as the Purchases and Sales, with Nominal Codes:

Category Heading	Low	High
Staff Salaries	7003	7003
Employers N.I.	7006	7006
Rent	7100	7100
Rates	7103	7103
Electricity	7200	7200
Petrol	7300	7300
Motor Repairs	7301	7301
Postage	7501	7501
Telephone	7502	7502
Stationery	7504	7504
Cleaning	7801	7801
Bank Charges	7901	7901
Depreciation	8000	8099
Advertising	8200	8200
Insurance	8204	8204
Sundry Expenses	8206	8206

Check by ticking against your Trial Balance to ensure all the Sales, Purchases and Expenses have been entered. The remaining Trial Balance items should be entered on the Balance Sheet.

On completion, press ESC and proceed to 12.2.

12.2 Balance Sheet

At the end of the first month we can produce a Balance Sheet, showing everything that the firm owns and owes at the month end.

    Choose NOMINAL LEDGER from the Main Menu
    Choose NOMINAL ACCOUNT STRUCTURE from the Sub-Menu
    Choose BALANCE SHEET

Just as for the Trading and Profit and Loss Account, we have to set up the parameters for the computer.

A Balance Sheet is split up into four sections:

    FIXED ASSETS
    CURRENT ASSETS
    CURRENT LIABILITIES
    FINANCED BY

The Fixed Assets will include accounts such as Plant and Machinery, Fixtures and Fittings, Motor Vehicles etc.

Under Fixed Assets, enter the following under the category headings, low and high parameters, and delete any other items:

Category Heading	Low	High
Lease	0011	0011
Depreciation Lease	0012	0012
Motor Van	0050	0050
Van Depreciation	0051	0051

The Current Assets should include accounts such as Closing Stock, Debtors Control, Bank Account (if we are not overdrawn) and any Cash.

Stock Clothes	1001	1001
Stock Sportswear	1002	1002
Stock Household	1003	1003
Debtors	1100	1100
Sundry Debtors	1103	1103
Petty Cash	1230	1230

The Current Liabilities should include accounts such as Creditors Control, Sundry Creditors, Bank (if overdrawn), VAT, PAYE and N.I. owing.

Creditors	2100	2100
Sundry Creditors	2109	2109
PAYE and N.I.	2210	2211
VAT	2200	2201
Bank Overdraft	1200	1200

Finally, the Financed By section of the Balance Sheet:

Capital	3000	3000
Retained Profit/Loss	3200	3200

After setting all the parameters, you can now extract a full set of final accounts at the end of the first month.

To do this:

> Choose MONTHLY ACCOUNTS from the Sub-Menu
> Choose PROFIT & LOSS and BALANCE SHEET

The program will then begin sorting through the information. You will be prompted to insert a disk for 'Last Month.' As this is your first month, ignore this and press ENTER.

You should now get a printout of the final accounts for 'This Month' and 'The Year to Date' (in this case identical).

If the Balance Sheet does not balance, recheck carefully that all the items in the TRIAL BALANCE have been entered in the monthly account.

Unit 13: Month end procedures

The program provides the facility for comparing actual performance with a BUDGET FORECAST. The forecast or budget figures can be entered as the nominal ledger is set up (see 2.1), or they can be entered separately as follows;

> Choose NOMINAL LEDGER from the menu
> Choose NOMINAL ACCOUNT STRUCTURE
> Choose ACCOUNT LIST

Now choose the required nominal code i.e. 4000 SALES CLOTHES
Yearly budget: enter £37000
Now copy the budget figures from the next page.
Month 1 £2800, Month 2, Month 3 etc.
To total £37000

Complete this procedure for every coded item only.

In order to check the figures have been correctly entered:

> Choose BUDGET REPORT enter month 12 and print.

The year to date column should equal the total budget figures shown on the handwritten budget on page 46.

To produce the BUDGET REPORT the same method is used as for producing the MONTHLY ACCOUNTS. The BUDGET REPORT will enable you to compare the actual results against the budgeted figures.

13.1 Budget Report

Choose MONTHLY ACCOUNTS from the Main Menu
Choose BUDGET REPORT from the Sub-Menu

You will be asked for a 'Month No.' but as this is your first month's postings

ENTER 1 and press ENTER
Choose PRINT or FILE
Enter [P]

Switch on printer and press ENTER

A full BUDGET REPORT will then be printed showing the monthly and cumulative figures compared to the budget, including variances in figures and percentages.

See BUDGET FIGURES on the following page

13.2 End of Period Report

At the end of the month it is possible to produce a variety of reports from each of the ledgers.

13.3 Sales Ledger Reports

AGED ACCOUNTS

From the Sales Ledger you should produce a list of balances at the month end. This report will show you the turnover, the credit limit, and the current balance for each of the Sales Ledger Accounts. By pressing the arrow button you can find out the aged analysis of each account so that outstanding accounts can be progressed.

To do this:

Choose SALES LEDGER
Choose ACCOUNT BALANCES (AGED)
Lower Account Reference [enter]
Upper Account Reference [enter]
Date of report   310194
Display print or file [print]

BUDGET FIGURES

FAMILY FAVOURITES BUDGET 1992

	A/c	TOTAL	JAN	FEB	MAR	APR	MAY	JUNE	JLY	AUG	SEP	OCT	NOV	DEC
SALES														
CLOTHES	4000	37000	2800	2500	3700	2700	2400	3000	2500	2700	3500	2300	2200	6200
SPORTSGOODS	4001	57000	4100	3900	5300	4000	4300	6000	3700	3000	6000	4700	4400	8600
HOUSEHOLD	4002	46000	3700	3400	4400	3500	3300	4000	3300	3000	5000	3700	4000	4800
TOTAL SALES		140000	10600	9800	13400	10200	10400	13000	9500	8700	14500	10700	10800	19600
PURCHASES														
CLOTHES	5000	16300	1700	1100	1600	1700	1300	1300	1100	1200	1500	1000	1000	2800
SPORTSGOODS	5001	31400	2300	2200	3000	2300	2400	2800	2400	1700	3400	2700	3200	5000
HOUSEHOLD	5002	29700	2400	2300	1900	2300	2100	2700	2400	2000	3400	2500	2700	3700
TOTAL PURCHASES		78400	6900	6605	7500	5800	5800	6800	5400	4900	8300	6200	6700	10000
GROSS PROFIT		61600	4700	4400	5900	4400	4600	5200	4100	3800	6200	4500	4700	9600
Less EXPENDITURE														
WAGES	7003	20500	1524	1524	1905	1524	1524	1905	1630	1630	2038	1630	1630	2036
NATIONAL INSURE	7004	676	52	52	52	52	52	65	52	52	65	52	52	65
RENT	7100	5750	479	479	479	479	479	479	479	479	479	479	479	481
RATES	7103	3000	250	250	250	250	250	250	250	250	250	250	250	250
STATIONERY	7504	150	12.5	12.5	12.5	12.5	12.5	12.5	12.5	12.5	12.5	12.5	12.5	12.5
INSURANCE	8204	700	58	58	58	58	58	58	58	58	58	58	58	58
MOTOR REPAIRS	7301	1700	85	85	85	85	85	85	85	85	58	85	85	67
PETROL	7300	2500	100	100	100	100	100	100	100	100	100	100	100	100
ELECTRICITY	7200	1500	208	208	208	208	208	208	208	208	208	208	208	212
ADVERTISING	8200	2800	167	167	147	83	88	93	83	83	83	147	108	167
BANK CHARGES	7901	500	214	196	890	702	802	210	190	174	260	214	212	349
TELEPHONE	7502	200	47	47	47	47	47	47	47	47	47	47	47	38
POSTAGE	7501	200	17	17	17	17	17	17	17	17	17	17	17	13
CLEANING	7801	240	20	23	20	20	20	20	20	20	20	20	20	20
SUNDRY EXPENSES	8204	300	25	25	25	25	25	25	25	25	25	25	25	25
		240	20	20	20	20	20	20	20	20	20	20	20	20
DEPRECIATION :-														
LEASE	8000	1000	83	83	83	83	83	83	83	83	83	83	83	87
VAN	8003	1250	104	104	104	104	104	104	104	104	104	104	104	104
TOTAL EXPENDITURE		41606	3373.5	3257.5	3823.5	3281.5	3285.5	3711.5	3673.5	3457.5	3844.5	3481.5	3473.5	4088.5
NET PROFIT		19994	1315.5	843.5	2076.5	1118.5	1314.5	1488.5	746.5	4442.5	2305.5	1018.5	910.5	5513.5

TRANSACTION HISTORY

You can produce or examine the details of what has happened on any one or every account in the sales ledger.

To do this:

> Choose SALES LEDGER
> Choose TRANSACTION HISTORY
> Lower Account Reference [Blank] for Blankley
> Upper Account Reference [Blank]
> Display Print or file [print]

To print out the total transactions for the period you simply select [enter] after reference.

DAY BOOKS

Day books can be produced to show the monthly list of the Sales Ledger invoices and credit notes (including VAT), and receipts and discounts.

To do this:

> Choose SALES LEDGER
> Choose DAY BOOKS

and select which option you require. If you wish to select the January items only you will need to enter the lower transaction as a number [34] and ENTER for the upper transaction.

STATEMENTS

The programme will produce statements for either all or any one of the sales ledger accounts. The programme can be set up to print your address on a prepared statement or you can design your own. Your technician may need to help you with this although full details are included in the SAGE manual.

To do this for Blankley:

> Choose SALES LEDGER
> Choose STATEMENTS
> Lower Account   [blank]
> Upper Account   [blank]
> Print or file   [print]
> Individually   [Y]
> Your address   [Y]

You will notice that you can include a three line message on the statement.

LETTERS

You can also produce a standard letter automatically for overdue accounts or where the credit limit has been exceeded.

To do this:

> Choose SALES LEDGER
> Choose LETTERS and select which option you require.

13.4 Purchase Ledger Reports

Exactly the same information can be can be produced for the purchase ledger except remittance advices will be provided instead of statements for payment details.

13.5 Nominal Ledger Reports

For nominal ledger reports you must choose NOMINAL LEDGER:

Choose TRIAL BALANCE

for an up to date print out.

Choose TRANSACTION HISTORY

for details of any or all Nominal Ledger Accounts.

Choose DAY BOOKS

for details of the bank payments and bank receipts and details of the cash payments and cash receipts. A detailed list of all the journals can be also produced from this option.

The MANAGEMENT REPORTS have already been explained.

13.6 Audit Report

Finally, having entered all the data for the period, it is necessary to produce a complete list of your postings for audit purposes.

To do this:

Choose UTILITIES from the Main Menu
Choose AUDIT TRAIL from the Sub-Menu
Print or file [print]
Enter

IMPORTANT NOTICE!

The month's cycle has now been completed. Make sure that you take at least one copy on disk of your transactions so far and clearly label it with the date and details.

Unit 14: Stock Control

Having completed all the transactions for January you can now proceed to enter the data for February. In this month Mr Sims, the proprietor, wishes to introduce more items onto the computer. He wants to introduce stock control and automatic sales invoicing. Also, at the end of February his next VAT payment is due. He asks you to complete the second month's transactions and then prepare the VAT Return and the Management Reports for 'Month 2', February 1994.

14.1 Setting up the Stock Control System

Continue with your original disk and from the menu:

Choose STOCK CONTROL
Choose CATEGORIES

Select the following CATEGORY NUMBERS

Category 1   Type in CLOTHES
Category 5   Type in SPORTSWEAR
Category 10   Type in HOUSEHOLD

Escape to stock control menu

14.2 Stock details

Now, using the stock list on page 50, enter the stock details at the 1st of February as follows:

Choose   UPDATE STOCK DETAILS
Enter   STOCK CODE
Type   DESCRIPTION
Enter   CATEGORY
Enter   SALE PRICE
Unit of Sale   EACH
Enter   NOMINAL CODE
Escape

14.3 Opening Stock Balances

The next step is to enter the opening stock balances at the beginning of February (see page 50).

Choose   ADJUSTMENTS IN
Enter   STOCK CODE
Enter   QUANTITY
Enter   COST PRICE (AVERAGE COST)
Narrative   OPENING STOCK
Reference   O/BAL
Date   01/02/94

Return to the Sub-Menu and on completion of this task print out a STOCK VALUATION. You can now compare it to the opening stock valuation to see if it agrees. If so proceed to the next stage, if not investigate the differences.

STOCK REPORTS - STOCK VALUATION

Category 1 CLOTHES All Nominal Codes 4000

Stock Code	Description	Quantity in Stock	Unit Cost	Stock Value	Selling Price
0201	Three Piece Suit	46	£9.10	£418.60	£19.99
0202	Embroidered Cotton Dress	30	£5.90	£177.00	£12.99
0203	Beach Dress	45	£4.54	£204.30	£9.99
0402	Pleat Front Trousers	10	£5.90	£59.00	£12.99
0504	Brushed Cotton Sweatshirt	35	£4.54	£158.90	£9.99
0505	Three Piece Office Suit	14	£13.63	£190.82	£29.99
0704	White Bikini	22	£7.00	£154.00	£13.99
				£1362.62	

Category 5 SPORTSWEAR All Nominal Codes 4001

Stock Code	Description	Quantity in Stock	Unit Cost	Stock Value	Selling Price
1001	Hang Ten Jacket	10	£15.00	£150.00	£29.99
1002	Long John wet Suits	10	£15.00	£150.00	£39.99
1105	Sweatshirts	25	£4.50	£112.50	£14.99
1106	Adidas Shorts	12	£4.50	£54.00	£8.99
1107	Grey Sweatshirt	15	£5.50	£82.50	£10.99
1108	Jog Pants	40	£7.00	£280.00	£13.99
1109	Red Sweatshirt	20	£8.50	£170.00	£17.99
1110	Blue Polo Shirts	30	£5.00	£150.00	£9.99
1401	Pilot Fitness Shoes	20	£12.50	£250.00	£24.99
1402	Continental Fitness Shoe	20	£18.50	£370.00	£36.99
1403	Jack Running Shoes	20	£14.00	£280.00	£27.99
1404	Sydney Running Shoes	20	£13.00	£260.00	£25.99
				£2309.00	

Category 10 HOUSEHOLD All nominal Codes 4002

Stock Code	Description	Quantity in Stock	Unit Cost	Stock Value	Selling Price
4908	Goblin Cleaner	7	£36.75	£257.25	£54.99
4906	Steam Iron	2	£14.60	£29.20	£21.99
5201	50 Piece Household Set	3	£25.30	£75.90	£37.99
5401	30 Piece Dinner Set	14	£9.30	£130.20	£13.99
5402	12 Piece Tea Set	20	£6.75	£135.00	£9.99
5403	18 Piece Tea Set	15	£9.25	£138.75	£13.99
5601	Kenwood Chef	14	£66.00	£924.00	£99.99
5602	Liquid Attachment	10	£10.00	£100.00	£15.99
5604	Food Processor	1	£50.00	£50.00	£74.99
5605	Kenwood Oven	8	£43.25	£346.00	£64.99
5606	Kenwood Toaster	10	£13.25	£132.50	£19.99
5603	Mincer	0	£0.00	£0.00	£19.99
5607	Kenwood Jug Kettle	2	£13.25	£26.50	£19.99
				£2345.30	

14.4 February Goods inwards and Purchases and Purchase Returns

Enter GOODS INWARDS into stock by updating the STOCK CONTROL RECORDS.

Choose	STOCK CONTROL
Choose	ADJUSTMENTS IN

From the Purchase Invoices for February 1994 (see pages 52–53)

Enter	THE STOCK CODE
Enter	THE QUANTITY
Check	THE PRICE and adjust it if necessary
Narrative	TYPE IN GOODS INWARDS
Reference	ENTER SUPPLIERS CODE REFERENCE
Enter	THE INVOICE DATE
Escape	

For new items not previously entered refer to 14.2 and 'Update Stock Details'.

14.5 Purchase Returns

For goods returned out of stock (page 54):

Choose	ADJUSTMENTS OUT
Enter	THE STOCK CODE
Enter	QUANTITY
Enter	COST PRICE
Narrative	RETURNED GOODS
Reference	ENTER SUPPLIERS CODE
Date	As credit note
Escape	

14.6 Purchase Invoices and Credit Notes

Once all these items have been entered into stock, enter the Purchase Invoices and Credit Notes as before (see 4.2).

In practice always use a Batch Control Slip.

Choose	PURCHASE LEDGER
Choose	BATCHED DATA ENTRY
Choose	INVOICES

To check these entries ESCAPE to Purchase Ledger. Check the number of entries at the top of the screen and deduct the last seven entries.

Choose	DAY BOOKS
Choose	PURCHASE INVOICES
Choose	LOWER TRANSACTION NUMBER
Choose	UPPER TRANSACTION NUMBER
Enter	

Enter Date Range from 010294 to 290294 and PRINT.

BETTERWARES

7 Sutton Way, Sutton Coldfield, West Midlands.

Invoice

To :
Family Favourites
Lichfield Rd Ind Est
Tamworth
Staffs

Customer Order Number :	Despatched by :	Invoice no :	Invoice Date / Tax Point :
FF 245		4567	1/2/94

Cat Number :	Quantity :	Description :	Price :	£	p
5201	2	50 pc household set	25.30	50	60
5402	10	12 pc household set	6.75	67	50
5403	10	18 pc tea set	9.25	92	50
5605	2	Compact oven	43.25	86	50
5606	10	Toaster	13.25	132	50
5607	2	Jug Kettle	13.25	26	50
5202	4	Pressure Cooker	18.66	74	64

	£	p
Gross Value of Goods	530	74
Less Discount		
Net Value of Goods		
Plus V.A.T. @ 17.5%	92	87
Invoice total	623	61

E & O E

Terms :   V.A.T. Registration No :

Mann Richards

Unit 4, Brigetown Ind. Est. Bridgetown, Walsall.

To :
Family Favourites
Lichfield Rd Ind Est
Tamworth
Staffs

Invoice

Customer Order Number :	Despatched by :	Invoice No :	Invoice Date / Tax Point :
FF 220		1999	2/2/94

Cat Number :	Quantity :	Description :	Price :	£	p
4908	2	Goblin Cleaner	36.75	73	50
5601	5	Kenwood Chef	66.00	330	00
5602	5	Liquidiser attachment	10.00	50	00
5603	2	Mincer	13.50	27	00
5604	1	Food Processor	50.00	50	00
5203	6	5 piece Pan Set	20.00	120	00

	£	p
Gross Value of Goods	650	50
Less Discount		
Net Value of Goods		
Plus V.A.T. @ 17.5%	113	84
Invoice total	764	34

E & O E

Terms :   V.A.T. Registration No :

Nikey

75 London Road
Leicester

Invoice

To :
Family Favourites
Lichfield Rd Ind Est
Tamworth
Staffs

Customer Order Number :	Despatched by :	Invoice no :	Invoice Date / Tax Point :
FF210		7822	15/2/94

Cat Number :	Quantity :	Description :	Price :	£	p
0704	30	B&W Bikini	7.00	210	00
1001	20	Hang Ten Jacket	15.00	300	00
1002	20	Long John Wet suit	20.00	400	00
1105	30	Sweatshirts	4.50	135	00
1108	20	Jog Pants	7.00	140	00
1109	10	Red sweatshirt	8.50	85	00

	£	p
Gross Value of Goods	1270	00
Less Discount		
Net Value of Goods		
Plus V.A.T. @ 17.5%	222	25
Invoice total	1492	25

E & O E

Terms :   V.A.T. Registration No :

Levis

3 Broad Street,
Birmingham.

Invoice

To :
Family Favourites
Lichfield Rd Ind Est
Tamworth
Staffs

Customer Order Number :	Despatched by :	Invoice no :	Invoice Date / Tax Point :
FF202		P2345	9/2/94

Cat Number :	Quantity :	Description :	Price :	£	p
0504	20	Brush Cott Sweat Shirt	4.54	90	80
0201	20	3 pce. suit	9.10	182	00

	£	p
Gross Value of Goods	272	80
Less Discount		
Net Value of Goods		
Plus V.A.T. @ 17.5%	47	74
Invoice total	320	54

E & O E

Terms :   V.A.T. Registration No :

Racquets & Balls

26 New Invention,
Walsall.

Invoice

To :	Family Favourites Lichfield Rd Ind Est Tamworth Staffs					

Customer Order Number : FF150	Despatched by :	Invoice No : PI 776	Invoice Date / Tax Point : 5/2/94		

Cat Number :	Quantity :	Description :	Price :	£	p
1105	5	Sweatshirt	4.50	22	50
1107	10	Grey sweatshirt	5.50	55	00
1110	10	Blue Polo Shirts	5.00	50	00
1401	25	Pilot fitness shoes	12.50	312	50
1402	20	Continental fitness shoes	18.50	370	00
1403	20	Jack running shoe	14.00	280	00
1404	20	Sydney running shoe	13.00	260	00
1106	24	Adidas Shorts	4.50	108	00

		Gross Value of Goods	1458	00
		Less Discount		
		Net Value of Goods		
		Plus V.A.T. @ 17.5%	255	15
E & O E		Invoice total	1713	15

Terms :	V.A.T. Registration No. :

Britannia

Unit 4, Green Lane, Cannock.

Invoice

To :	Family Favourites Lichfield Rd Ind Est Tamworth Staffs					

Customer Order Number : FF200	Despatched by :	Invoice no : 9210	Invoice Date / Tax Point : 7/2/94		

Cat Number :	Quantity :	Description :	Price :	£	p
0202	15	Sundress	5.90	88	50
0203	70	Peach dress	4.54	317	80
0402	20	Pleat front trousers	5.90	118	00
0505	20	Suit & 2 skirts	13.63	272	60

		Gross Value of Goods	796	90
		Less Discount		
		Net Value of Goods		
		Plus V.A.T. @ 17.5%	139	46
E & O E		Invoice total	936	36

Terms :	V.A.T. Registration No :

Mann Richards

Unit 4, Brigetown Ind. Est. Bridgetown, Walsall.

To :	Family Favourties Lichfield Rd Ind Est Tamworth Staffs			**Invoice**		

Customer Order Number : FF 220	Despatched by :	Invoice no : 2004	Invoice Date / Tax Point : 3/2/94		

Cat Number :	Quantity :	Description :	Price :	£	p
5603	3	Mincer	13.50	40	50
4906	6	Steam Iron	14.60	87	60
5202	4	Pressure Cooker	18.66	74	64

		Gross Value of Goods	202	74.
		Less Discount		
		Net Value of Goods		
		Plus V.A.T. @ 17.5%	35	48
E & O E		Invoice total	238	22

Terms :	V.A.T. Registration No :

Mann Richards

Unit 4, Brigetown Ind. Est.
Bridgetown, Walsall.

Credit Note

Family Favourites Lichfield Rd Ind Est Tamworth Staffs			Vat Reg. No. Date : 27/2/94	
Reason for Credit	Quantity and Description	Total credit (Excluding V.A.T.)	V.A.T. Credited	
			Rate	Amount
Broken	1 Liquidiser attachment 5602	10.00	17.5%	1.75 £11.75

Credit Note

Levis

3 Broad Street, Birmingham.

Credit Note

Family Favourites Lichfield Rd Ind Est Tamworth Staffs			VAT Reg. No. Date : 15/2/94	
Reason for Credit	Quantity and Description	Total credit (Excluding V.A.T.)	V.A.T. Credited	
			Rate	Amount
Holes in back	2 Brush cotton sweat 0504	9.08	17.5%	1.60 £10.68

Credit Note

Unit 15: Automatic invoicing

Mr Sims is now satisfied that the stock systems are satisfactory for his needs and he wishes to try the automatic invoicing. To do this you need to ensure that your program has been correctly set up to use the default stationery.

15.1 Automatic Invoices

Family Favourites existing manual invoice system relies on sales invoices being typed directly from the customers order. This order is used to pick and deliver the goods and it is important to include this number on the INVOICE so that the delivery can be matched by the customer. Note that the Stock Number used for identifying the goods should be included in the description. Often goods are not in stock and this results in several invoices needing to be retyped. Mr Sims is keen to try out the Automatic Invoice System and asks you to process the typed invoices for February to see how the system works.

Invoices and credit notes can be generated from the Sage Sterling program itself and then the ledgers updated automatically.

All items are priced individually, so ignore UNITS item.

15.2 Invoice Production

An invoice or credit note consists of three sections:

HEADING
STOCK ITEMS
FOOT ITEMS

To enter an Invoice:

Choose SALES LEDGER
Choose INVOICE PRODUCTION from the Main Menu
Choose INVOICING FROM STOCK from the Sub-Menu

HEADING

The invoice number will be automatically allocated and the cursor will be positioned over the Date field.

If you want to change the invoice number, press the UP ARROW key to position the cursor over the invoice number and re-enter the new number.

Enter your first invoice No. 9001

If you enter a number from an existing invoice, the details will be retrieved from file and displayed on the screen.

You will be expected to enter details alongside the following screen prompts:

DATE: Enter date of invoice
SALES REF: Enter Customer's code. (i.e. BLANK)

The customer's name and address will automatically be retrieved from the Sales Ledger.

DELIVERY NAME/ADDRESS:

You can type in an alternative address if the goods are to be delivered elsewhere.

CUSTOMER ORDER NO:

If you have an order number put it in here.

The remaining details on the HEADING screen are all updated by the program and cannot be altered on the screen.

To move to the next screen, press the Page Down key [Pg Dn].

STOCK ITEMS

Press ENTER.

Now complete the following areas for the first item on the invoice.

STOCK CODE
QUANTITY
UNITS (EACH)
DISCOUNT 10%
TAX CODE T1
NOMINAL CODE

Press [Pg Dn]

If there is a second item on the invoice you can now enter the details for it on this screen and continue until you have completed all the items for that customer.

Press [Pg Dn] to move to the footing part of the invoice.

FOOT ITEMS

Here you can enter up to three lines of additional notes that relate to the whole invoice. These can be printed on the invoice or can be used for reference purposes only.

Now CHECK.

When you have completed the relevant details on this screen, press the ESC key and the program will return to the HEADING screen.

Now check to see if after completion this invoice agrees with the typed invoice, if different EDIT and correct errors.

To save an invoice on file, press the ESC key when you are on the HEADING screen and the following question will appear at the top right hand corner of the screen:

Do you want to   Save   Edit   Abandon?

Press ENTER to Save.

A new screen will appear to complete another invoice. If you have finished entering invoices and want to return to the Invoice Production Menu, press ESC.

You can now enter the Sales Invoices on pages 57–59 and, where necessary, alter the quantities. The program will advise you where there is insufficient stock and you can revise the delivery and send out what stock you have (see Unit 16).

FAMILY FAVOURITES

Lichfield Road Industrial Estate, TAMWORTH

Invoice

To: Mrs E Whitehouse
26 Thorne Rd
Sutton Coldfield
West Midlands

Customer Order Number :	Despatched by :	Invoice No :	Invoice Date / Tax Point :
2137B	Van	9003	7/2/94

Cat Number :	Quantity :	Description :	Price :	£	p
5607	3	Jug Kettle	19.99	59	97
5603	5	Mincer	19.99	99	95
5605	2	Compact oven	64.99	129	98

	Gross Value of Goods	289	90
	Less Discount	28	99
	Net Value of Goods	260	91
	Plus V.A.T. @ 17.5%	45	66
E & O E	Invoice total	306	57

Terms :   V.A.T. Registration No. : 84362957

FAMILY FAVOURITES

Lichfield Road Industrial Estate, TAMWORTH

Invoice

To: Mrs C Evans
42 Oak View
Rugeley
Staffs

Customer Order Number :	Despatched by :	Invoice No :	Invoice Date / Tax Point :
8181A	Rail	9004	12/2/94

Cat Number :	Quantity :	Description :	Price :	£	p
1401	10	Pilot Fitness Shoes	24.99	249	90
1402	8	Continental Fitness Shoes	36.99	295	92
1403	5	Jack Fitness Shoes	27.99	139	95
1404	10	Sydney Fitness Shoes	25.99	259	90

	Gross Value of Goods	945	67
	Less Discount	94	56
	Net Value of Goods	851	11
	Plus V.A.T. @ 17.5%	148	94
E & O E	Invoice total	1000	05

Terms :   V.A.T. Registration No. : 84362957

FAMILY FAVOURITES

Lichfield Road Industrial Estate, TAMWORTH

Invoice

To: Mr A Holloway
The Fairings
Four Oaks
West Midlands

Customer Order Number :	Despatched by :	Invoice No :	Invoice Date / Tax Point :
Phone 3/2/92	Van	9002	4/2/94

Cat Number :	Quantity :	Description :	Price :	£	p
0402	10	Pleat-front-trousers	12.99	129	90
0505	10	Suit + 2 skirts	29.99	299	90

	Gross Value of Goods	429	80
	Less Discount	42	98
	Net Value of Goods	386	82
	Plus V.A.T. @ 17.5%	67	70
E & O E	Invoice total	454	52

Terms :   V.A.T. Registration No. : 84362957

FAMILY FAVOURITES

Lichfield Road Industrial Estate, TAMWORTH

Invoice

To: Mrs T Blankley
5 Ingold Ave
Walsall
West Midlands

Customer Order Number :	Despatched by :	Invoice No :	Invoice Date / Tax Point :
14710	Van	9001	3/2/94

Cat Number :	Quantity :	Description :	Price :	£	p
0201	20	3 pc suit	19.99	399	80
0202	25	Sundress	12.99	324	75
0203	30	Beachdress	9.99	299	70

	Gross Value of Goods	1024	25
	Less Discount	102	42
	Net Value of Goods	921	83
	Plus V.A.T. @ 17.5%	161	32
E & O E	Invoice total	1083	14

Terms :   V.A.T. Registration No. : 84362957

FAMILY FAVOURITES

Lichfield Road Industrial Estate, TAMWORTH

Invoice

To: Mr P Weir
32 Cedar Rd
Cannock
Staffs

Customer Order Number :	Despatched by :	Invoice No :	Invoice Date / Tax Point :
1414D	Rail	9007	24/2/94

Cat Number :	Quantity :	Description :	Price :	£	p
4906	4	Mann Richards Iron	21.99	87	96
4908	2	Cylinder Cleaner	54.99	109	98
5202	2	Pressure Cooker	27.99	55	98
5401	2	30 pc dinner set	13.99	27	98
5601	2	Kenwood Chef	99.99	199	98

			£	p
		Gross Value of Goods	481	88
		Less Discount	48	19
		Net Value of Goods	433	68
		Plus V.A.T. @ 17.5%	75	90
E & O E		Invoice total	509	58

Terms :   V.A.T. Registration No. : 84362957

FAMILY FAVOURITES

Lichfield Road Industrial Estate, TAMWORTH

Invoice

To: Miss J Goldingay
71 Chiltern Rd
Wolverhampton
West Midlands

Customer Order Number :	Despatched by :	Invoice No :	Invoice Date / Tax Point :
Phone 15/2/94	Van	9006	18/2/94

Cat Number :	Quantity :	Description :	Price :	£	p
5602	1	Liquidiser attachment	15.99	15	99
5606	12	Toaster	19.99	239	88
5203	3	5 pc pan set	27.99	83	97
5402	15	12 pc tea set	9.99	149	85
5403	5	18 pc tea set	13.99	69	95
4906	2	Mann Richards Iron	21.99	43	98

			£	p
		Gross Value of Goods	603	62
		Less Discount	60	36
		Net Value of Goods	543	26
		Plus V.A.T. @ 17.5%	95	07
E & O E		Invoice total	638	33

Terms :   V.A.T. Registration No. : 84362957

FAMILY FAVOURITES

Lichfield Road Industrial Estate, TAMWORTH

Invoice

To: Mrs J Williams
3 The Avenue
Polesworth
Tamworth, Staffs

Customer Order Number :	Despatched by :	Invoice No :	Invoice Date / Tax Point :
141/FF	Van	9008	27/2/94

Cat Number :	Quantity :	Description :	Price :	£	p
0704	30	B & W Bikini	13.99	419	70
1001	5	Hang Ten	29.99	149	95
1002	5	Wet Suit	39.99	199	95
1105	30	Mens Running Vests	14.99	449	70

			£	p
		Gross Value of Goods	1219	30
		Less Discount	121	90
		Net Value of Goods	1097	40
		Plus V.A.T. @ 17.5%	192	05
E & O E		Invoice total	1289	45

Terms :   V.A.T. Registration No. : 84362957

FAMILY FAVOURITES

Lichfield Road Industrial Estate, TAMWORTH

Invoice

To: Mrs M Harris
Sevenoaks
Long Lane
Lichfield
Staffs

Customer Order Number :	Despatched by :	Invoice No :	Invoice Date / Tax Point :
1718C	Van	9005	15/2/94

Cat Number :	Quantity :	Description :	Price :	£	p
0504	35	Brush cotton Sweatshirt	9.99	349	65
0505	10	Suit + 2 skirts	29.99	299	90
0402	15	Pleat front trousers	12.99	194	85
0203	25	Beachdress	9.99	249	75
0202	15	Sundress	12.99	194	85

			£	p
		Gross Value of Goods	1289	00
		Less Discount	128	90
		Net Value of Goods	1160	10
		Plus V.A.T. @ 17.5%	203	02
E & O E		Invoice total	1363	12

Terms :   V.A.T. Registration No. : 84362957

FAMILY FAVOURITES

Lichfield Road Industrial Estate, TAMWORTH

Invoice

To: Mr P. Weir
32 Cedar Rd
Cannock
Staffs

Customer Order Number :	Despatched by :	Invoice No :	Invoice Date / Tax Point :
9101D	Rail	9011	27/2/94

Cat Number :	Quantity :	Description :	Price :	£	p
1401	20	Pilot Fitness Shoes	24.99	499	80
1404	40	Sydney Runnings Shoes	25.99	1039	60
		Gross Value of Goods		1539	40
		Less Discount		153	94
		Net Value of Goods		1385	46
		Plus V.A.T. @ 17.5%		242	46
E & O E		Invoice total		1627	92

Terms :   V.A.T. Registration No. : 84362957

FAMILY FAVOURITES

Lichfield Road Industrial Estate, TAMWORTH

Invoice

To: Mr A Holloway
The Fairings
Fours Oaks
West Midlands

Customer Order Number :	Despatched by :	Invoice No :	Invoice Date / Tax Point :
Phone 20/2	Rail	9010	28/2/94

Cat Number :	Quantity :	Description :	Price :	£	p
1106	24	Adida Shorts	8.99	215	76
1105	25	Sweat Shirts	14.99	374	75
1108	20	Jog Pants	13.99	279	80
		Gross Value of Goods		870	31
		Less Discount		87	03
		Net Value of Goods		783	28
		Plus V.A.T. @ 17.5%		137	07
E & O E		Invoice total		920	35

Terms :   V.A.T. Registration No. : 84362957

FAMILY FAVOURITES

Lichfield Road Industrial Estate, TAMWORTH

Invoice

To: Mrs A Nolan
14 Hatherton Street
Cheslyn Hay
West Midlands

Customer Order Number :	Despatched by :	Invoice No :	Invoice Date / Tax Point :
2408	Rail	9009	28/2/94

Cat Number :	Quantity :	Description :	Price :	£	p
1001	15	Hang ten	29.99	449	85
1002	15	Wet suit	39.99	599	85
1106	10	Adidas Shorts	8.99	89	90
1107	15	Mens sweat shirts	10.99	164	85
1108	20	Jogging Pants	13.99	279	80
1109	15	Mens sweat shirts	17.99	269	85
		Gross Value of Goods		1854	10
		Less Discount		185	41
		Net Value of Goods		1668	69
		Plus V.A.T. @ 17.5%		291	97
E & O E		Invoice total		1960	66

Terms :   V.A.T. Registration No. : 84362957

Unit 16: Printing Invoices & Updating Ledgers

16.1 Update Ledgers

When you generate an invoice from the Sage program, it is not automatically posted to the ledger.

To post invoices to the ledger, and to reduce the stock:

> Choose INVOICE PRODUCTION from the Main Menu
> Choose UPDATE LEDGERS from the Sub-Menu

Again you will be prompted for the upper and lower invoice numbers.

If you want to update all invoices press ENTER.

A complete list of the invoices updated will then be produced. If an invoice cannot be updated through lack of stock or no price etc. the programme will inform you so that you may go back to check the invoice details. If there is insufficient stock you can send what you can and alter your invoice accordingly.

To do this, go back to INVOICE PRODUCTION and redirect the invoices not updated. Make a note of the stock codes and quantities in question and then ESCAPE and save and exit from the Sales Ledger to the Main menu.

> Choose STOCK CONTROL
> Choose STOCK HISTORY

Go through the stock ledger until you come to the stock item in question. Is there sufficient stock to send? If not, decide what can be sent and then go back to the Sales Ledger. Again choose INVOICES PRODUCTION and alter the invoices in question accordingly. Escape and UPDATE LEDGERS again for the invoice in question.

Retry the DISPLAY INDEX to see if all the invoices have been posted and if [yes] you can now print them out (as shown in 16.3).

16.2 Invoice Index

The invoice display index gives a list of all invoices generated by the system and gives details of whether they have been posted and/or printed.

> Choose INVOICE PRODUCTION from the Main Menu
> Choose DISPLAY INDEX from the Sub-Menu

Are all the invoices displayed?

16.3 Invoice Printing

To print any or all of the invoices or credit notes:

> Choose INVOICE PRODUCTION from the Main Menu
> Choose PRINT INVOICES from the Sub-Menu

You will then be prompted for upper and lower invoice numbers if you only want a few. Alternatively, if you want to print all invoices, just press ENTER.

Free Text invoice	N
Input File Name	Enter
Ignore Printed Flag	N
Print or File	P
Pause between Pages	Y

Invoices can only be printed once.

Before you attempt to print invoices it is recommended that you check the invoices are correct and update them if necessary as in 16.1.

16.4 Stock Valuation

Ensure that the Cash Sales Invoice Numbers 84 and 85 are adjusted out of stock before producing the stock valuation (see 18.6).

To do this:

> Choose STOCK CONTROL
> Choose ADJUSTMENTS OUT

and enter the Cash Sale Details

Narrative	CASH SALES
Reference	CASH
Date	as Invoice

Once this has been done and the entries for Modules 14, 15 and 16 have been entered, the stock valuation for the end of February can be produced.

> Choose STOCK CONTROL
> Choose STOCK VALUATION

Now Print out a valuation by category and by code to use as your closing stock in the February Monthly Accounts.

The Sage Financial Controller Programme has an integrated Sales and Purchase order system which is ideal for this type of business. The proprietor intends to introduce this in the following month.

Unit 17: Other February Entries

The remaining entries for February (pages 62–66) can now be entered. Using the experience gained from entering the first month's transactions, you will need to decide which ledger you should enter these February items in.

Firstly, enter the expenses paid by cheque: telephone, wages and rent etc. (see Unit 7, for help if necessary). For the February Wage Journal you should refer to Unit 8.

Next you will need to enter the cheques paid to suppliers (see as previous Unit 5.2) and then cheques received from customers (see as previous Unit 5.1).

Finally the Cash Payments and Receipts (page 68) can be entered and the cash float restored to the required £200 level.

CASH TRANSFER

Refer to Unit 6 for January and calculate the necessary amount to obtain from the bank to make up the Cash Float balance to £200.00.

Then Choose JOURNAL ENTRIES and make the necessary Journal as follows:

> Debit Cash Account
> Credit Bank Account

On completion of this Unit, a new Bank Reconciliation should be prepared and you should take out a new Trial Balance prior to completion of the Month End Adjustments.

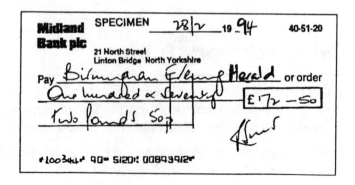

ADAM FORD GARAGE

Upper Gungate, Tamworth.

Family Favourites,
Lichfield Rd Ind Est.,
Tamworth,
Staffs.

Date : 28.02.94

	£
130 gallons of petrol at £1.48 per gallon	192.40
V.A.T. @ 17.5%	33.67
TOTAL	226.07

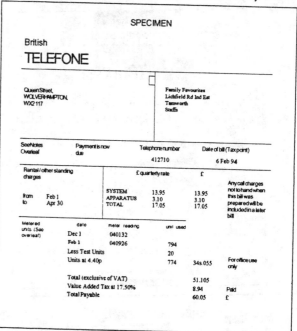

British

TELEFONE

Queen Street,
WOLVERHAMPTON,
WX2 117

Family Favourites
Lichfield Rd Ind Est
Tamworth
Staffs

See Notes Overleaf	Payment is now due	Telephone number	Date of bill (Tax point)
		412710	6 Feb 94

Rental / other standing charges		£ quarterly rate	£	Any call charges not to hand when this bill was prepared will be included in a later bill
from Feb 1	SYSTEM	13.95	13.95	
to Apr 30	APPARATUS	3.10	3.10	
	TOTAL	17.05	17.05	

Metered units (See overleaf)	date	meter reading	unit used		For office use only
	Dec 1	040132			
	Feb 1	040926	794		
Less Test Units			20		
Units at 4.40p			774	34s.055	
Total (exclusive of VAT)				51.105	
Value Added Tax at 17.50%				8.94	Paid
Total Payable				60.05	£

Midland Bank plc SPECIMEN 28/2 19 94 40-51-20

21 North Street
Linton Bridge, North Yorkshire

Pay *Adam Ford* _____ or order

two hundred + twenty   £226-07

six pounds 07 pence

R Sims.

100345' 90" 5120: 00893912"

Midland Bank plc SPECIMEN 15/2 19 94 40-51-20

21 North Street
Linton Bridge North Yorkshire

Pay *British Telefone* _____ or order

sixty pounds 05   £60 — 05

R Sims

100343 90 5120: 00806912

BS	Standing Order Mandate

To : Midland Bank Ltd.

Address : 21 North Street, Linton Bridge, North Yorkshire.

	bank	Branch title (not address)	Code number
Please Pay	T.S.B.	Lichfield	30-08-27

	Beneficiary	Account Number
for the credit of	Grabber Properties	1 3 7 0 5 6 2

	Amount in figures	Amount in words
the sum of	479.17	Four hundred and seventy nine pounds

	Date and amount of 1st payment		Date and frequency
commencing	1/8/92	And thereafter every	4th of Month
	*now		

	Date and amount of last payment	
*until	Further notice	Machine operator please note this is monthly rent, code 7100

quoting the reference

* This instruction cancels any previous order in favour of the beneficiary named above, under this reference
* If the amount of the periodic payments vary they should be incorporated in a schedule overleaf

Special instructions

Signature :	*R Sims*	Date	1/8/93

Title and number of account to be debited	Family Favourites Ltd	6 1 0 2 1 3 9 7

Note : The bank will not undertake to

(i) make any references to Value Added Tax or pay a stated sum "plus VAT"

(ii) advise payer's addresses to beneficiary

(iii) advise beneficiary of inability to pay

(iv) request beneficiary's banker to advise beneficiary of receipt

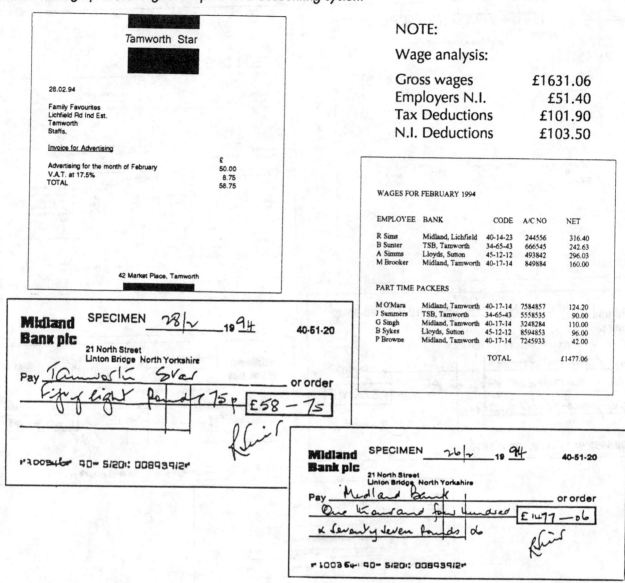

Tamworth Star

28.02.94

Family Favourites
Lichfield Rd Ind Est.
Tamworth
Staffs.

Invoice for Advertising

	£
Advertising for the month of February	50.00
V.A.T. at 17.5%	8.75
TOTAL	58.75

42 Market Place, Tamworth

NOTE:

Wage analysis:

Gross wages	£1631.06
Employers N.I.	£51.40
Tax Deductions	£101.90
N.I. Deductions	£103.50

WAGES FOR FEBRUARY 1994

EMPLOYEE	BANK	CODE	A/C NO	NET
R Sims	Midland, Lichfield	40-14-23	244556	316.40
B Sunter	TSB, Tamworth	34-65-43	666545	242.63
A Simms	Lloyds, Sutton	45-12-12	493842	296.03
M Brooker	Midland, Tamworth	40-17-14	849884	160.00

PART TIME PACKERS

M O'Mara	Midland, Tamworth	40-17-14	7584857	124.20
J Summers	TSB, Tamworth	34-65-43	5558535	90.00
G Singh	Midland, Tamworth	40-17-14	3248284	110.00
B Sykes	Lloyds, Sutton	45-12-12	8594853	96.00
P Browne	Midland, Tamworth	40-17-14	7245933	42.00
			TOTAL	£1477.06

Midland Bank plc SPECIMEN 28/ν 19 94   40-51-20

21 North Street
Linton Bridge North Yorkshire

Pay *Tamworth Star* or order
Fifty eight pounds 75p £58 — 75

⑈200346⑈ 90⑈ 5⑈20⑈: 00893912⑈

Midland Bank plc SPECIMEN 26/ν 19 94   40-51-20

21 North Street
Linton Bridge North Yorkshire

Pay *Midland Bank* or order
One thousand four hundred
& seventy seven pounds 06 £1477 — 06

⑈200364⑈ 90⑈ 5⑈20⑈: 00893912⑈

NOTE:

Payment of January Deductions form Wages

Code 2210	£102.94
Code 2211	£104.00

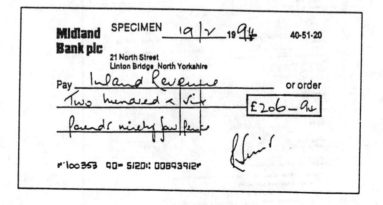

Midland Bank plc SPECIMEN 19/ν 19 94   40-51-20

21 North Street
Linton Bridge North Yorkshire

Pay *Inland Revenue* or order
Two hundred & six
pounds ninety four pence £206 — 94

⑈200353⑈ 90⑈ 5⑈20⑈: 00893912⑈

Cheque 1:

Midland Bank plc
SPECIMEN   15/2   19 94   40-51-20
21 North Street
Linton Bridge North Yorkshire
Pay   Racquet & Balls   or order
Two thousand one hundred   £2,116 - 18
& sixteen pounds 18p

r 100349 90= 5120: 00893912

Cheque 2:

Midland Bank plc
SPECIMEN   6/2   19 94   40-51-20
21 North Street
Linton Bridge North Yorkshire
Pay   Better Wares   or order
One thousand three hundred   £1315 - 02
fifteen pounds 02p

100347 90= 5120: 00893912

Cheque 3:

Midland Bank plc
SPECIMEN   21/2   19 94   40-51-20
21 North Street
Linton Bridge North Yorkshire
Pay   Brittania   or order
Eight hundred & seventy seven   £877 - 75
pounds 75p

r 100350 90= 5120: 00893912

Cheque 4:

Midland Bank plc
SPECIMEN   10/2   19 94   40-51-20
21 North Street
Linton Bridge North Yorkshire
Pay   Nikey   or order
Four thousand pounds   £4000 - 00
only

r 100352 90= 5120: 00893912

Cheque 5:

Midland Bank plc
SPECIMEN   26/2   19 94   40-51-20
21 North Street
Linton Bridge North Yorkshire
... Leeds.   or order
five hundred & thirty four   £534 - 16
pounds 16p

r 100348 90= 5120: 00893912

Cheque 6:

Midland Bank plc
SPECIMEN   3/2   19 94   40-51-20
21 North Street
Linton Bridge North Yorkshire
Pay   Mann Richards   or order
Six hundred & three   £603 - 72
pounds 72p

r 100351 90= 5120: 00893912

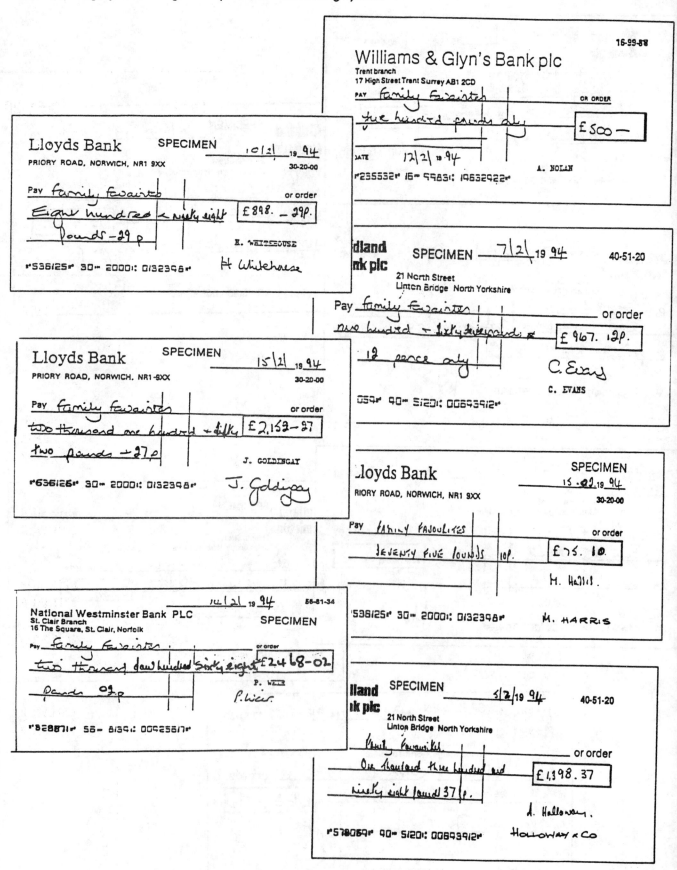

Statement of account with

Midland Bank plc

SPECIMEN 28 February   19 94   40-51-20

21 North Street
Linton Bridge North Yorkshire

Type of Account :   Name :   Account Number :

Current   Family Favourites   00893912

Date	Description	Withdrawals	Deposits	Balance
1.02.94	BROUGHT FORWARD			1016.16DR
1.02.94	Credits		786.18	
1.02.94	100337	63.25		
	100338	155.25		
	100339	231.60		
	100089	1498.06		
1.02.94	Credit		134.70	2043.44DR
2.02.94	S/O Grabber Prop	479.17		2522.61DR
6.02.94	100347	1315.02		3837.63DR
15.02.94	100348	534.16		
15.02.94	100351	603.72		
15.02.94	100352	4000.00		8975.51DR
17.02.94	100349	2116.18		11091.69DR
18.02.94	Credits		967.12	
20.02.94	Credits		575.10	
21.02.94	Credits		1398.37	8151.10DR
20.02.94	100343	60.05		8211.15DR
21.02.94	Credits		898.29	
22.02.94	Credits		4620.29	2692.57DR
28.02.94	100354	1477.06		
28.02.94	Bank Charges	30.21		
28.02.94	100353	206.94		
28.02.94	100350	877.75		5284.53DR
28.02.94	Returned Cheque	2468.02		7752.55DR

Details of rates and calculation of any interest charged are available on request from your
branch. Abbreviations: *Credit Balance DR Overdrawn Balance S Sub Total
(Intermediate Balance)

CASH PAYMENTS FEBRUARY

			£	
February	2	Petrol	23.00	(VAT Included)
	7	Milk	4.60	
	8	WHSmith (Stationery)	56.00	(VAT Included)
	10	Tea & Coffee	9.20	
	12	Window cleaner	23.00	
	15	Postage	35.00	
	17	Petrol	28.00	(VAT Included)
	28	Petrol	27.00	(VAT Included)
	27	Acto Auctions	1400.00	(VAT Included)
		(Second-hand Sewing Machine)		
		Month Total	1605.80	

CASH RECEIPTS

FAMILY FAVOURITES

Lichfield Road Industrial Estate, TAMWORTH

Atherstone Hardware
Atherstone
Warwicks

CASH SALE .85.   20/2/94

Ref	Description	Qty.	Unit Price		Total	
4908	Goblin 30 Cyl Cleaner	2	54	99	109	98
4906	Steam Iron	2	21	99	43	98
5201	50 Piece Household Set	3	37	99	113	97
5401	30 Piece Dinner Set	4	13	99	55	96
5604	Food Processor	1	74	99	74	99
	Total				£398	88
	Plus VAT 17.5%				£69	80
					£468	68

FAMILY FAVOURITES

Lichfield Road Industrial Estate, TAMWORTH

Fred Bloggs
(Sports Shop)
High St
Burton-on-Trent
Staffs   CASH SALE .84.   20/2/94

Ref	Description	Qty.	Unit Price		Total	
1107	Grey Sweatshirt	10	10	99	109	90
1108	Jog Pants	20	14	99	299	80
1109	Red sweatshirt	10	17	99	179	90
1110	Blue Polo Shirt	25	9	99	249	75
	Total				£839	35
	Plus VAT 17.5%				£146	89
					£986	24

Unit 18: Adjustment for Returned Cheques, Repayments, and Contra Entries

After the preparation of the preliminary Trial Balance for February the following adjustments will need to be taken into consideration before you can complete the month end accounts.

18.1 Returned Cheques

The company has received a letter from the Bank dated 28th February 1994 to say that a cheque from WEIR dated 14th February 1994 has been returned marked 'insufficient funds'. This means that the cheque has bounced and you will need to amend the company records as follows:

Choose	SALES LEDGER
Choose	REFUNDS
Choose	CANCEL CHEQUES
Enter	the appropriate account reference [WEIR]
Select	the cheque to cancel by entering the shaded area
Do you wish to post [enter]	

The sales ledger is updated to resurrect the debt as though the cheque had not been posted. It also automatically adjusts the bank account.

18.2 Repayments

Exactly the same action is required for repayments or refunds for both Purchase and Sales Ledgers.

18.3 Contra Entries

A contra entry would normally be required when a supplier is also a customer, and the balance of one ledger is set off against the other. In order to demonstrate the procedure required, you may assume that Harris has collected some materials direct from Nikey which we invoiced to him for £301.18. Nikey has already charged for these items in their outstanding balance for £899.32

The procedure requires you to firstly to pay the difference through the purchase ledger by raising a cheque for Nikey No 100361 for £598.14. This must be allocated as a part-payment.

To execute the contra:

Choose	SALES LEDGER
Choose	CONTRA

Enter the accounts codes for both sales and purchase ledger accounts. Now you can select the amount to contra by entering the shaded area above both amounts for £301.18. Both ledgers will be automatically updated.

18.4 Bad Debt Write off

A letter dated 28th February has been received from the Receivers of Whitby suggesting that it is most unlikely that there will be any payments to creditors. Your Manager therefore asks you to write off the debt in this months accounts.

To do this:

Choose	SALES LEDGER
Choose	BAD DEBT WRITE OFF
Choose	WRITE OFF ACCOUNT

Enter the customer's Code and the full details of the Account will be displayed. You will be asked whether to proceed with the write off; answer [YES].

The total amount written off will then be displayed and all the necessary transfers automatically carried out.

18.5 Bad Debt Provision

In view of the above experience your Manager has decided to make a provision against future bad debts. He asks you to make a provision for bad debts at 5% of the company's trade debtors. You will need to set up a new account for BAD DEBT PROVISION No 1104 and include it in the balance sheet structure in the Current Assets under Debtors. (Refer to Unit 2 and Unit 12.2 if required).

A journal entry must then be made through the Nominal Ledger to debit account 8102 and credit account 1104 for 5% of the final trade debtors.

18.6 February Month End Adjustments

Finally, you will need to complete the month end adjustments for February. (You are recommended to refer to Modules 9, 10, and 11 before attempting these items).

ADJUSTMENTS FOR CLOSING STOCK.

The closing stock figures for January must now be cancelled and the February stocks entered. To do this you need to make the journal entries on page 71 opposite those entered in Unit 9.1, and enter the closing stock entries for February using the calculations you completed in Unit 16.

CODE	DETAIL	ACCOUNT	DR £	CR £
1001	reverse entry	Clothes		1362.62
1002	reverse entry	Sportswear		2309.00
1003	reverse entry	Household		2345.00
5200	reverse entry	Clothes	1362.62	
5201	reverse entry	Sportswear	2309.00	
5202	reverse entry	Household	2345.00	
1001	closing stock	Clothes	1176.54	
1002	closing stock	Sportswear	1768.50	
1003	closing stock	Household	2534.21	
5200	closing stock	Clothes		1176.54
5201	closing stock	Sportswear		1768.50
5202	closing stock	Household		2534.21

ACCRUALS AND PREPAYMENTS.

A new prepayment for the rental of telephones should now be included. The amount of £17.05 should be entered as a prepayment in the Nominal Ledger by selecting PREPAYMENTS and entering the name of the account under the previous item. You should enter the nominal code as 7502, the value, and the period as 3 months.

DEPRECIATION

You will need to update the depreciation for the additional item of plant and machinery. This is the sewing machine purchased in February for cash. You will need to select DEPRECIATION and enter the nominal code for PLANT AND MACHINERY DEPRECIATION as 0021, enter the value and set the straight line depreciation of machinery at 12.5%.

When you have completed these month end activities you can update them automatically with your previous entries by using the month end facility in the UTILITIES IN THE MAIN MENU (see Units 10.3 and 11.2). At the same time the Stock Balances can be set up for March by also following the month end routine.

FINAL TRIAL BALANCE

You will now need to return to the NOMINAL LEDGER to take out a final trial balance for February. Before you proceed with the February Accounts you should check that you have updated the Profit and Loss Account and Balance Sheet NOMINAL ACCOUNT STRUCTURE to cater for any new accounts used for the first time this month (see Unit 12).

A careful check from the Trial Balance to NOMINAL ACCOUNT STRUCTURE for any accounts not entered may save you the problem of a Balance Sheet that does not balance. You can now proceed with your Month End reports for February.

LIQUIDITY RATIO

An additional report to those already entered is the LIQUIDITY RATIO.

If you want to check the company's liquidity:

Choose NOMINAL LEDGER
Choose QUICK RATIO
Do you want to VIEW or EDIT?
Choose [EDIT]

Now list the Current Assets

N/C	ACCOUNT
1001	Stock Clothes
1002	Stock Sportswear
1003	Stock Household
1100	Debtors Control
1200	Bank Current Account
1230	Petty Cash
2100	Creditors Control
2200	Tax Control
2210	PAYE
2211	National Insurance

Now you can [Escape] and go back to [VIEW].

Display or Print to show the totals of the Current Assets and Current Liabilities. A healthy liquidity should show Debits exceeding Credits by 2:1

Unit 19: VAT Returns

The program contains the facility for producing the figures required for the VAT RETURNS. On completion of the February data, the VAT report can be produced as follows:

Choose   NOMINAL LEDGER from the Main Menu
Choose   VAT RETURN ANALYSIS from the Sub-Menu
Enter   Transaction No.(1) Lower Transaction No.
Enter   Transaction No.(?) Last Transaction No. for February.
Enter   Data Range 01.01.94 to 28.02.94
Enter   [P] to Print Out.

The report will show the total inputs and outputs for each Tax Code. The total T1 outputs less the total T1 tax inputs should be the amount payable to the Customs and Excise.

To check the total output and input tax:

Choose   CONTROL ACCOUNTS HISTORY
Choose   TAX CONTROL
Enter   Lower Transaction No [1]
Enter   Upper Transaction No [?]

and Print.

The balance of the Control Account should agree with the net Tax in VAT Return Analysis. Any difference must be investigated and reconciled. You may find that the difference is due to a date error on posting a transaction.

After agreement the balance of the VAT account should be transferred by Journal to Account 2201 (VAT Liability). A cheque for this amount can then be made out to CUSTOMS & EXCISE to clear this Liability.

You can now complete the VAT return on page 74:

    Enter the T1 Outputs in column [1]
    Enter the T1 Inputs in column [2]
    Enter the difference in column [3]

In order to complete the columns [4] and [5], you will need to add the following output and input figures for December 1993 to the net output and input figures on the Tax Analysis Summary:

    Net output of December 1993   £11416.73
    Net Input for December 1993   £9878.60

Unit 20: Report Generator

Using the Report Generator, you can design and produce your own reports using any of the details held in the accounts data disk. You can select which information is to appear on a report, the order in which it will be printed, specify which columns are to be totalled and where to 'break' the report and produce sub-totals. Not only that, but you can also request that a particular report is sorted on a particular piece of information, e.g. sort alphabetically on customer name, sorted by turnover-to-date, etc.

Calculations can be included in any report. You may use addition, subtraction multiplication and division of any two or more fields in a section to produce the information required.

Each field can have a selection criteria applied to them. This enables tests to be made on the field, e.g. Turnover greater than £2000, Balance not equal to 0, etc.

Finally, you can either send the report to a printer, store it on file for printing later or output it in a form suitable for a database or mailmerge to read.

The Report Generator has been included in all of the 'report' options on the 'Main' menu. For example, to design a report within the Sales Ledger:

    Choose REPORT GENERATOR from the Main Menu
    Choose SALES LEDGER REPORTS from the Sub-Menu

When you enter the Report Generator, a list of all reports created previously will be displayed on the screen along with their title.

Only eight reports can be shown at once. If you have more than eight reports within a particular section, only the first eight will be displayed on the screen. The others, although not shown on the screen, are still accessible.

If you want to enter a new layout, enter a new name alongside the prompt 'Report Name' and press RETURN.

Value Added Tax Return
For the period
01.12.93 to 28.2.94

Registration number	Period
843-62957	02

You could be liable to a financial penalty if your completed return and all the VAT payable are not received by the due date.

Due date:

For official use DOR only

Family Favourites
Lichfield Industrial Estate
Tamworth
Staffordshire

Your VAT Office telephone number is

Fold here

Before you fill in this form please read the notes on the back and the VAT Leaflet *"Filling in your VAT return"*. Complete all boxes clearly in ink, writing 'none' where necessary. Don't put a dash or leave any box blank. If there are no pence write "00" in the pence column. Do not enter more than one amount in any box.

For official use			£	p
	VAT due in this period on sales and other outputs	**1**		
	VAT reclaimed in this period on purchases and other inputs	**2**		
	Net VAT to be paid to Customs or reclaimed by you (Difference between boxes 1 and 2)	**3**		
	Total value of sales and all other outputs excluding any VAT. Include your box 6 figure	**4**		
	Total value of purchases and all other inputs excluding any VAT. Include your box 7 figure	**5**		
	Total value of all sales and related services to other EC Member States	**6**		
	Total value of all purchases and related services from other EC Member States	**7**		

Retail schemes. If you have used any of the schemes in the period covered by this return please enter the appropriate letter(s) in this box.

If you are enclosing a payment please tick this box.

DECLARATION by the signatory to be completed by or on behalf of the person named above.

I, ... declare that the
(Full name of signatory in BLOCK LETTERS)
information given above is true and complete.

Signature .... Date .... 19 ......

A false declaration can result in prosecution.

The report you are about to design will be stored under this filename and can be recalled at any time. If you need to modify the report or if you want to update it when more details have been added to the datadisk, simply recall the file using the appropriate filename.

Payroll Section

This Payroll Package is a supplement to the Computerised Accounts Package, specially designed for use with Sage Sterling Payroll II Software

Introduction

A separate Sage payroll program is required for the Payroll Section. This programme can be installed within the Sterling range without difficulty by following the Sage Installation Guide

As with the accounting programs, there is a considerable amount of work involved in installing payroll records. It is essential that the initial information is carefully and correctly entered. You will find that the benefits come later with automatic calculation of wages, tax and National Insurance and the cumulative record keeping for the Inland Revenue.

The next eight modules deal with our small company's attempts to transfer its payroll to the computer for the months of March and April. These months were selected deliberately in order to give you the experience of the Tax Year End Returns and setting up the records for the new Tax Year.

Getting Started

Configuration

After installation of the Payroll II programme choose PAYROLL from the SAGE STERLING MENU and key in your first Payroll date as 31/3/94. The main PAYROLL MENU will then be displayed to you on the screen as follows:

```
PAYROLL MENU

EMPLOYEE DETAILS
PROCESSING PAYROLL
STATUTORY SICK PAY
STATUTORY MATERNITY PAY
GOVERNMENT PARAMETERS
COMPANY DETAILS
```

To move around the PAYROLL MENU use the arrow keys on the number pad or the Home and End keys. When you are positioned above the menu item you want to select press [enter].

When you wish to finish using the programme *always return to the STERLING menu and select QUIT*. This will ensure that your data has been saved on the data disk. You can always return to the main menu by selecting the ESCAPE [Esc] key.

Before you can begin to process any payroll data it is necessary to first check that the tax and insurance details are correct.

GOVERNMENT PARAMETERS

The Sage Payroll II is supplied with tax and national insurance details already entered. These details need to be checked with up to date GOVERNMENT PARAMETERS to ensure the correct rates are being used. The tax used in this particular example is the tax year 1993/1994. To do this select the PAYROLL PROGRAMME from the main SAGE STERLING MENU and Enter:

Choose GOVERNMENT PARAMETERS from the payroll menu
Choose TAX BANDWIDTHS AND RATES from the sub menu

The screen will now show you the tax bandwidths contained in the programme which may need adjustment to bring it up to date. To do this enter the range for 1993/94 in pounds and then the % tax applicable, but first alter the number of bandwidths to [2].

TAX BANDWIDTH		FROM	TO	TAX
1	£2500	£0.01	£2500.00	20%
2	£21200	£2500.00	£23700.00	25%
3	£excess	£23700.00	'EXCESS'	40%

The number of BANDWIDTHS can be changed by altering the 'No of Bandwidths' field [Enter]. To move around the screen use the arrows and HOME and END keys.

Next, you can carry out the same exercise for National Insurance Bandwidths, National Insurance Categories, National Insurance Rates, SSP Parameters, SSP Rates and SMP Rates. The number of bandwidths should be [4].

Choose National Insurance Rates and enter:

NATIONAL INSURANCE CONTRIBUTIONS			
Lower		to	£56.00
Band 1	£56.00	to	£94.99
Band 2	£95.00	to	£139.99
Band 3	£140.00	to	£194.99
Band 4	£195.00	to	£420.00
Over	£420.00		

```
STATUTORY SICK PAY

THRESHOLD      FROM        TO

1      £56        £56      £194.99
2      £195       £195     EXCESS
```

```
STATUTORY MATERNITY PAY

LOWER RATE      £47.95
HIGHER RATE     90% of average earnings for first 6 weeks
```

For further information you may need to refer to the PAYROLL II USER MANUAL.

Unit 21: Setting up the Records

21.1 The Company Details

The first information you are required to enter are details about your company.

To do this:

> Choose COMPANY DETAILS from the menu and enter
> Choose COMPANY INFORMATION and enter

Family Favourites company information is as follows:

Bank Name	MIDLAND BANK PLC
Address	21 NORTH STREET
	LINTON BRIDGE YORKSHIRE
Sort Code	40-51-20
Account Name	FAMILY FAVOURITES
Account Number	00893912
Tax Reference	FF 464/327
Cash Rounding	0.00
Retirement	Age
Women	60
Men	65

Enter the above information in the areas provided and then press [Esc] to return to the company menu.

21.2 Pension Schemes

Now choose PENSION RATES to enter details of any company pension schemes. Family Favourites have just one pension scheme for management only. The scheme requires a 5% contribution from the employer and a similar contribution from the employee. Enter these percentages under the % column against number 1. Note that up 10 schemes could be provided for.

The second section allows up to four separate contracted out pension schemes (Scheme Contracted Out Numbers). This section should only be used for schemes that have been contracted out since January 1986.

Finally, the third section requires a single entry to show whether the pension amount will receive full tax relief. Enter [y] for tax relief and for this particular company enter [n] for no tax relief.

21.3 Cash Analysis Limits

If your company wishes to determine the type of bank notes or coin used in cash payroll payments this option allows you to decide by

Choose CASH ANALYSIS from the Sub-Menu

Entering the value 9999 in the £50 or £20 will prevent bank notes of these denominations being used in the payroll.

Entering [0] in all the fields will make the programme attempt to use all denominations in the most effective way.

21.4 Department Names

Up to twenty DEPARTMENT NAMES can be accommodated by the programme. If you wish to analyse the company wages by department:

Choose DEPARTMENT NAMES from the sub menu and enter:

1. MANAGEMENT

2. ADMINISTRATION

3. SALES

4. PACKING

Now press [Esc] to return to the company details.

21.5 Payment Types

Different types of employees are sometimes paid in different ways. Some may receive a straight monthly salary, others may be paid at an hourly rate.

This option allows you to select up to 10 methods of payment:

Choose PAYMENT TYPES from the sub menu
Enter 1. SALARY
         2. BASIC RATE
         3. OVERTIME
Press [Esc] and return to the company details.

21.6 Adjustment Types

A similar option is available for ADJUSTMENTS to the payroll. Up to 20 fields are available to adjust the payment by addition or subtraction. For this example only bonus will need to entered for this option:

Choose   ADJUSTMENT TYPES from the Sub-Menu and
enter   1. BONUS
Enter [y]   (if this adjustment is to be considered for tax and N I)
Enter [n]   (if not)
Press [Esc] and return to company details.

21.7 Parameters Listing

Selection of this option will enable you to either print, file, or view the completed list of company details. You will be able to check all the details you have entered and refer to the list as necessary.

Choose PARAMETERS LISTING from the Sub-Menu
[p] print [f] file or [v] view.

Unit 22: Employee Details

22.1 Employee Details

The EMPLOYEE DETAILS option allows you to enter and amend the personal details of your payroll. It is a laborious task which needs to be done carefully. Once completed these records can be used for every payroll.

Before getting started on this activity it is important to realise that the EMPLOYEE DETAILS are split into 'FOUR PAGES' which can be accessed by the arrow keys or [PG UP] or [PG DN].

The first page contains:

```
PERSONAL DETAILS
Employee Number
Name and Address
Type of Payment
Pension Reference
Auto SSP/SMP
Date of Birth
Start Date
Tax Codes
Effective From
N.I. Number and Category
SCON Reference
Marital Status
Male /Female
Director
```

The next page contains:

```
WAGE TABLE SELECTIONS
Department Number
Qualifying Days
Rates of Pay
Adjustments
```

The third page will contain:

```
BANK/P45 INFORMATION
Details of Bank Account
Previous P45 Details
Gross Pay NI (Directors Only)
```

The final page will show the cumulative totals for the year to date for gross pay, tax and N.I. These figures will be taken from the totals on the company's P11 Forms.

22.2 Employee Records

As you are using the system for the first time it is necessary to set up the individual payroll details.

Do this as follows:

> Choose EMPLOYEE DETAILS and enter
> Choose ADD A NEW EMPLOYEE and enter

Now enter the personal details of your payroll as contained on the next pages, pressing [page down] to complete each page.

BANK INFORMATION/P45

Next you must enter the BANK INFORMATION/P45

[Page Down] to BANK INFORMATION/P45 and enter the Bank information.

If you are entering a new employees details part way through the TAX YEAR it is important to put the taxable gross earnings to date and the tax paid in the [taxable gross pay P45] and the total [tax paid], otherwise ignore this item.

The gross pay for NI is only required for to calculate National Insurance Contributions for directors, so ignore this option and [page down].

CUMULATIVE VALUES

Finally the CUMULATIVE VALUES for the year to date need to be entered unless you are using the programme at the beginning of the tax year. Using the information for each employee, enter all the required details for Family Favourites for NI Earnings, NI Contributions and Pensions. You can check the P11 documents, (Unit 3), to make sure you understand where this information came from.

There are no details for Holiday Pay, S.S.P., S.M.P. or Adjustments to be entered at this stage.

When you have entered the cumulative details for Roger Sims press [F10] twice and you will be asked to [Post, Edit or Abandon]. select [Post] and the next employees details can then be entered.

On completion of this task it is important to review each employees details to make sure your entries are correct before attempting your first payroll.

> Escape to return to the [EMPLOYEE DETAILS]

Next, to enter this information:

> Choose PROCESSING PAYROLL
> Choose PAYROLL RUN DATE at 28 February 1994
> Is this correct?   [Yes]
> Process   [Monthly]
> OK to process   [Enter]
> Clear Payments file   [Yes]

Now:

> Choose UPDATE RECORDS and enter.

Reference : 1	Name : ROGER BRIAN SIMS	Pay Type : GM

Employee No. : 1	Start Date	: 050493
Forenames : ROGER BRIAN	Leave Date	:
Surname : SIMS	Tax Code	: 525H
Address : 49 ASH ROAD	Effective from	: 050491
TAMWORTH	N.I. Number	: ZM106271A
STAFFORDSHIRE	N.I. Category	: A
B79 8MN	Contracted Out	: N
Works Number : 000001	SCON Ref.	: 0
Payment Type : GM	Effective From	: 050493
Pension Ref. : 1	Marital Status	: M
Auto SSP/SMP : Y	Male/Female	: M
Date of Birth : 291248	Director	: N

Page Down ▼

Department No : 1	Rate No	: 1 £712.00
Qualifying Days : 1	Adjustment No	: 1 BONUS

Page Down ▼

Bank Name : Midland Bank plc	Sort Code	: 40-14-32
Address : Lichfield,	Account Name	: R. B. & V. Sims
Staffordshire	Account No	: 244556

Page Down ▼

Cumulative Values	Current Employment	Year to Date	Employer
Total Gross Pay :	£8637.60	£8637.60	NI. : £742.61
Taxable Gross Pay :	£8637.60	£8637.60	Pension : £431.88
Tax paid :	£837.41	£839.41	
Std NI Earnings :	£8637.60		
NI Contributions :	£590.04		
Pension :	£431.88		

Reference : 2	Name : BARBARA MARY SUNTER	Pay Type : GM

Employee No. : 2	Start Date	: 050493
Forenames : BARBARA MARY	Leave Date	:
Surname : SUNTER	Tax Code	: 344L
Address : 1 MAYFIELD	Effective from	: 050493
ATHERSTONE	N.I. Number	: TL718203L
WARWICKSHIRE	N.I. Category	: A
CV26 34J	Contracted Out	: N
Works Number : 000002	SCON Ref.	: 0
Payment Type : GM	Effective From	: 050493
Pension Ref. : 0	Marital Status	: M
Auto SSP/SMP : Y	Male/Female	: F
Date of Birth : 120137	Director	: N

Page Down ▼

Department No : 1	Rate No	: 2 £2.50
Qualifying Days : 1	Adjustment No	: 1 BONUS

Page Down ▼

Bank Name : T.S.B.	Sort Code	: 35-65-43
Address : Tamworth,	Account Name	: Mrs B Sunter
Staffordshire	Account No	: 666543

Page Down ▼

Cumulative Values	Current Employment	Year to Date	Employer
Total Gross Pay :	£2894.76	£2894.76	NI. : £126.57
Taxable Gross Pay :	£2894.76	£2894.76	Pension : NIL
Tax paid :	NIL	£839.41	
Std NI Earnings :	£2894.76		
NI Contributions :	£82.76		
Pension :	NIL		

Reference : 3	Name : ALAN ALBERT SIMMS	Pay Type : GM

Employee No. : 3	Start Date : 050493
Forenames : ALAN ALBERT	Leave Date :
Surname : SIMMS	Tax Code : 79L
Address : 71 STONEY LANE	Effective from : 050493
LICHFIELD	N.I. Number : ZX442107T
STAFFORDSHIRE	N.I. Category : A
	Contracted Out : N
Works Number : 000003	SCON Ref. : 0
Payment Type : GM	Effective From : 050493
Pension Ref. : 0	Marital Status : S
Auto SSP/SMP : Y	Male/Female : M
Date of Birth : 290352	Director : N

Department No : 3	Rate No : 1 £650.00
Qualifying Days : 1	Adjustment No : 1 BONUS

Bank Name : Lloyds Bank plc	Sort Code : 45-12-12
Address : High Street, Lichfield	Account Name : A. A. Simms
Staffordshire	Account No : 493842

Cumulative Values	Current Employment	Year to Date	Employer
Total Gross Pay :	£7128.72	£7128.72	NI. : £613.93
Taxable Gross Pay :	£7128.72	£7128.72	Pension : NIL
Tax paid :	£1474.06	£1474.06	
Std NI Earnings :	£7128.72		
NI Contributions :	£455.40		
Pension :	NIL		

Reference : 4	Name : MARION BROOKER	Pay Type : GM

Employee No. : 4	Start Date : 050493
Forenames : MARION	Leave Date :
Surname : BROOKER	Tax Code : 344L
Address : 6 MAXSTOKE ROAD	Effective from : 050493
BELGRAVE	N.I. Number : TZ012234S
TAMWORTH	N.I. Category : A
STAFFORDSHIRE	Contracted Out : N
Works Number : 000004	SCON Ref. : 0
Payment Type : GM	Effective From : 050493
Pension Ref. : 0	Marital Status : M
Auto SSP/SMP : Y	Male/Female : F
Date of Birth : 221049	Director : N

Department No : 2	Rate No : 1 £695.00
Qualifying Days : 1	Adjustment No : 1 BONUS

Bank Name : Midland Bank plc	Sort Code : 40-17-17
Address : Church Street	Account Name : B & M Brooker
Tamworth	Account No : 894884

Cumulative Values	Current Employment	Year to Date	Employer
Total Gross Pay :	£7626.63	£7626.63	NI. : £677.60
Taxable Gross Pay :	£7626.63	£7626.63	Pension : NIL
Tax paid :	£991.25	£991.25	
Std NI Earnings :	£7626.63		
NI Contributions :	£476.96		
Pension :	NIL		

```
┌─────────────────────────────────────────────────────────────────────────┐
│  Reference : 5          Name : MAUREEN OMARA              Pay Type : GM   │
└─────────────────────────────────────────────────────────────────────────┘
```

Employee No. :	5	Start Date :	050493
Forenames :	MAUREEN	Leave Date :	
Surname :	OMARA	Tax Code :	344L
Address :	11 LACEY ROAD	Effective from :	050493
	EPWORTH	N.I. Number :	LM213172L
	STAFFORDSHIRE	N.I. Category :	A
		Contracted Out :	N
Works Number :	000005	SCON Ref. :	0
Payment Type :	GM	Effective From :	050493
Pension Ref. :	0	Marital Status :	S
Auto SSP/SMP :	Y	Male/Female :	F
Date of Birth :	150872	Director :	N

Department No :	4	Rate No :	1 £480.00
Qualifying Days :	1	Adjustment No :	1 BONUS

Bank Name :	Midland Bank plc	Sort Code :	40-17-17
Address :	Church Street	Account Name :	Miss M OMara
	Tamworth	Account No :	758857

Cumulative Values	Current Employment	Year to Date	Employer
Total Gross Pay :	£5640.00	£5640.00	NI. : £372.46
Taxable Gross Pay :	£5640.00	£5640.00	Pension : NIL
Tax paid :	£495.67	£495.67	
Std NI Earnings :	£5640.00		
NI Contributions :	£320.76		
Pension :	NIL		

```
┌─────────────────────────────────────────────────────────────────────────┐
│  Reference : 6          Name : JONATHON SUMMERS           Pay Type : GM   │
└─────────────────────────────────────────────────────────────────────────┘
```

Employee No. :	6	Start Date :	050493
Forenames :	JONATHON	Leave Date :	
Surname :	SUMMERS	Tax Code :	344L
Address :	11 LICHFIELD ROAD	Effective from :	050493
	TAMWORTH	N.I. Number :	TL332172K
	STAFFORDSHIRE	N.I. Category :	A
		Contracted Out :	N
Works Number :	000006	SCON Ref. :	0
Payment Type :	GM	Effective From :	050493
Pension Ref. :	0	Marital Status :	S
Auto SSP/SMP :	Y	Male/Female :	M
Date of Birth :	270370	Director :	N

Department No :	2	Rate No :	2 £2.65
Qualifying Days :	1	Adjustment No :	1 BONUS

Bank Name :	Midland Bank plc	Sort Code :	40-17-17
Address :	Church Street	Account Name :	Mr J. Summers
	Tamworth	Account No :	758485

Cumulative Values	Current Employment	Year to Date	Employer
Total Gross Pay :	£3995.00	£3995.00	NI. : £184.69
Taxable Gross Pay :	£3995.00	£3995.00	Pension : NIL
Tax paid :	£166.68	£166.68	
Std NI Earnings :	£3995.00		
NI Contributions :	£174.24		
Pension :	NIL		

Reference : 7	Name : GHANJA SINGH	Pay Type : GM

Employee No.	:	7		Start Date	:	050493
Forenames	:	GHANJA		Leave Date	:	
Surname	:	SINGH		Tax Code	:	344L
Address	:	5 ALBERT STREET		Effective from	:	050493
		LICHFIELD		N.I. Number	:	TZ447122A
		STAFFORDSHIRE		N.I. Category	:	A
				Contracted Out	:	N
Works Number	:	000007		SCON Ref.	:	0
Payment Type	:	GM		Effective From	:	050493
Pension Ref.	:	0		Marital Status	:	S
Auto SSP/SMP	:	Y		Male/Female	:	M
Date of Birth	:	210675		Director	:	N

Department No	:	4	Rate No	:	2 £2.95
Qualifying Days	:	1	Adjustment No	:	1 BONUS

Bank Name	:	Midland Bank plc	Sort Code	:	40-17-17
Address	:	Church Street	Account Name	:	Ghanja Singh
		Tamworth	Account No	:	845788

Cumulative Values	Current Employment	Year to Date	Employer	
Total Gross Pay :	£5170.00	£5170.00	NI. :	£340.45
Taxable Gross Pay :	£5170.00	£5170.00	Pension :	NIL
Tax paid :	£401.68	£401.68		
Std NI Earnings :	£5170.00			
NI Contributions :	£277.20			
Pension :	NIL			

Reference : 8	Name : BENJAMIN SYKES	Pay Type : GM

Employee No.	:	8		Start Date	:	050493
Forenames	:	BENJAMIN		Leave Date	:	
Surname	:	SYKES		Tax Code	:	344L
Address	:	2 BARNSLEY STREET		Effective from	:	050493
		ATHERSTONE		N.I. Number	:	LM226613X
		WARWICKSHIRE		N.I. Category	:	A
				Contracted Out	:	N
Works Number	:	000008		SCON Ref.	:	0
Payment Type	:	GM		Effective From	:	050493
Pension Ref.	:	0		Marital Status	:	S
Auto SSP/SMP	:	Y		Male/Female	:	M
Date of Birth	:	130168		Director	:	N

Department No	:	4	Rate No	:	2 £3.20
Qualifying Days	:	1	Adjustment No	:	1 BONUS

Bank Name	:	Midland Bank plc	Sort Code	:	40-14-32
Address	:	High Street	Account Name	:	Mr B. Sykes
		Atherstone	Account No	:	845793

Cumulative Values	Current Employment	Year to Date	Employer	
Total Gross Pay :	£4512.00	£4512.00	NI. :	£206.91
Taxable Gross Pay :	£4512.00	£4512.00	Pension :	NIL
Tax paid :	£270.07	£270.07		
Std NI Earnings :	£4512.00			
NI Contributions :	£217.80			
Pension :	NIL			

Reference : 9	Name : PAULA ANN BROWNE		Pay Type : GM

Employee No. :	9	Start Date :	050493
Forenames :	PAULA ANN	Leave Date :	
Surname :	BROWNE	Tax Code :	344L
Address :	37 BROWNS LANE	Effective from :	050493
	LICHFIELD	N.I. Number :	LD011123Z
	STAFFORDSHIRE	N.I. Category :	A
		Contracted Out :	N
Works Number :	000009	SCON Ref. :	0
Payment Type :	GM	Effective From :	050493
Pension Ref. :	0	Marital Status :	S
Auto SSP/SMP :	Y	Male/Female :	F
Date of Birth :	121065	Director :	N

Department No :	2	Rate No :	2 £2.75
Qualifying Days :	1	Adjustment No :	1 BONUS

Bank Name :	Yorkshire Bank plc	Sort Code :	01-55-64
Address :	Station Drive	Account Name :	Miss P. Brown
	Lichfield	Account No :	194877

Cumulative Values	Current Employment	Year to Date	Employer	
Total Gross Pay :	£1974.60	£1974.60	NI. :	-
Taxable Gross Pay :	£1974.60	£1974.60	Pension :	-
Tax paid :	NIL	NIL		
Std NI Earnings :	£1974.60			
NI Contributions :	-			
Pension :	-			

IMPORTANT NOTE

Before processing the Payroll you must make sure your EMPLOYEE DETAILS are correct. Then follow the UPDATE RECORDS procedure as shown in Unit 22.2

Unit 23: Processing the payroll

23.1 Processing the Payroll

You are now in a position to enter the March payroll for Family Favourites.

To do this:

Choose PROCESSING PAYROLL form the sub-menu
Check the PAYROLL RUN DATE is correct at 31st March 1994

Is this correct?	[Yes]
Process	[Monthly]
Ok to process	[Enter]
Lower employee no	[1]
Upper employee No.	[9]
CLEAR PAYMENTS FILE	[yes] or [no]

If you select [NO] the entries used in the last payroll run will be re-entered. Therefore if the majority of employees are paid a fixed salary their last figures are already entered. Selecting [YES] will clear the file.

You are now in the PROCESSING PAYMENTS option:

Choose ENTER PAYMENTS and enter Roger Sims pay details;

Roger is paid a salary so enter 1 in the first column

Next [page down] to enter his year end bonus of £350.00

Now [page up] and you should find that Roger's tax, NI and pension have been automatically calculated.

Select [F4] and move on to employee number 2.

Barbara Sunter is paid a basic rate, so enter the number of hours worked in the first column. You will need to refer to the following Employee Details for all the remaining wage details. All the employees are to be given a bonus of 10% of their March payment.

NAME	TAX CODE	NI CAT.	RATE	BONUS
Mr Roger Brian Sims	525H	A	£712pm	£350
Mrs Barbara Sunter	344L	A	100Hrs at £2.50	10%
Mr Alan Simms	79L	A	£650pm	10%
Ms Marion Brooker	344L	A	£695pm	10%
Mrs Maureen OMara	344L	A	£480pm	10%
Mr Jonathon Summers	344L	A	120Hrs at £2.65	10%
Mr Ghanja Singh	344L	A	140Hrs at £2.95	10%
Mr Benjamin Sykes	344L	A	140Hrs at £3.20	10%
Ms Paula Ann Browne	344L	A	65Hrs at £2.75	10%

On completion of the payroll [Escape] and return to the sub-menu.

Choose PAYMENT SUMMARY and enter
Choose PRINT SAVE OR VIEW and enter [p]

The payroll will now be printed in three parts.

PART 1   will show the complete payroll with individual and total tax, NI, pension, SSP, SMP and additions.

PART 2   details the National Insurance Contributions.

PART 3   summarises the year to date.

CASH ANALYSIS

This option allows you to list any employees who are paid in cash and the net pay is broken down to the type of bank note and coin that go to make up the payment.

CHEQUE ANALYSIS

A report can be reproduced from this option to show the individual amounts paid to each employee and the total amount paid by cheque.

GIRO ANALYSIS

As Family Favourites are paying the payroll by GIRO it is now possible to print out the details for the month's figures.

To do this:

Choose GIRO ANALYSIS and enter

Select [P] for print and print out the payslips for each individual in the payroll.

PAYSLIPS

It is possible to choose this option to print out the payslips for each employee. To do this the programme must be set up to use the PAYSLIP.LAYOUT as detailed in the Sage Systems Manual Stationary Layouts. You can design you own payslips or use the Default Layout provided.

The same option is available to print out GIROS and CHEQUES. For more information refer to the User Manual.

COLLECTOR OF TAXES

By choosing this option you can select the type of information you require for the payment to the Inland Revenue:

Employee Number Range,
Tax Month/Week Range or
Date Range

UPDATE RECORDS

Finally once you are satisfied that the payroll has been correctly entered this option will update the records by adding it to the existing data in the files. The cumulative files P11 will be adjusted to include the latest payroll so that the next payroll can be run.

Before updating the Payroll it is normal operating practice to save the data by backing up the information on another floppy disk. This can be done as part of the following procedure

Choose   UPDATE RECORDS and enter
Payroll Date   31st March 1994
Tax Month   [12]
Monthly

It is most important that this option is completed to prevent employees records being altered after the payment has been made.

Records can be UPDATED ONCE ONLY for the payroll payment.

Unit 24: Year End Procedure

24.1 Year End Procedure

Having now completed the TAX YEAR for the Family Favourites' Employees it is now possible to produce the Tax Year Summary for both employees and the Inland Revenue. This is normally a hugely time consuming job for someone using a manual payroll system, but Sage Payroll 11 can help you do this in minutes rather than days!

To do this simply escape to the PAYROLL menu and go to the MAIN MENU:

Choose UTILITIES and enter
Choose YEAR END and enter
Choose PAYROLL and enter

24.2 P35 Year End Summaries

This option allows you to produce the required details for the Year End P35 Deduction Sheets. The total National Insurance Contributions, SSP, SMP and Income Tax deducted from the payrolls during the TAX YEAR will be printed out for you in the format required for Form P35.

You could now enter the required Year End Tax information on the P35 Extract overleaf.

P11 DEDUCTION FORM

Escape and choose P11 DEDUCTION FORM. You can also print out details totalling the P11 Forms and check each employees deduction working sheets with the manual records needed for completion of Unit III of Part 2.

As you have only completed one month's payroll records the benefits of a line system are not obvious, but next year, each employee's P11 forms and deduction sheet can be produced on a monthly basis.

P14/P60 CERTIFICATES

Escape and choose P14/P60 CERTIFICATES. This option will print out the P60 Forms for you. A test pattern allows you to correctly line up the Annual P60 Forms before printing them out.

CLEAR YEAR TO DATE TOTALS

Finally, in order to prepare for next years payrolls yet preserving the employees details, choose CLEAR YEAR TO DATE TOTALS.

WARNING!! Cumulative details will be set to ZERO.

Year End Company Tax Return (P35) Extract

Deductions Working Sheets

You should list below the individual *Deductions Working Sheets* (forms P11) which you have filled in during the year and which contain a figure under any of the headings.

You should prepare continuation sheets if there is not enough space to list all your employees. Enter only the figures for 'this employment'.

Employee's name Put an asterisk (*) beside the name if the person is a director	National Insurance contributions (NIC). Enter the total of employee's and employer's NIC	Statutory Sick Pay (SSP) paid	Statutory Maternity Pay (SMP)	Income tax deducted or refunded. Write 'R' beside amount to show a net refund
_____	£_____·___	£_____·___	£_____·___	£_____·___
_____	£_____·___	£_____·___	£_____·___	£_____·___
_____	£_____·___	£_____·___	£_____·___	£_____·___
_____	£_____·___	£_____·___	£_____·___	£_____·___
_____	£_____·___	£_____·___	£_____·___	£_____·___
_____	£_____·___	£_____·___	£_____·___	£_____·___
_____	£_____·___	£_____·___	£_____·___	£_____·___
_____	£_____·___	£_____·___	£_____·___	£_____·___
_____	£_____·___	£_____·___	£_____·___	£_____·___
_____	£_____·___	£_____·___	£_____·___	£_____·___

Calculation of National Insurance contributions and income tax now due

	National Insurance contributions (NIC)	Statutory Sick Pay (SSP) paid	Statutory Maternity Pay (SMP)	Income tax
Totals from this page (remember to deduct any amounts marked 'R')	A £_____·___	A £_____·___	A £_____·___	A £_____
Totals from continuation sheets	B £_____·___	B £_____·___	B £_____·___	B £_____
Totals (A+B)	C £_____·___	C £_____·___	C £_____·___	C £_____
Received from the Inland Revenue to pay SSP or SMP	D £_____·___			
Total SSP recovered (1991-92 onwards) - see your *Employer's Payment Record* (form P32) or your *Payslip Booklet* (form P30BC) *		SSP recovered E £_____		
NIC compensation on SSP (only complete if form is used for 1990-91 or earlier) **	F £_____			
NIC compensation on SMP - see your *Employer's Payment Record* (form P32) or your *Payslip Booklet* (form P30BC)			G £_____	
Received from the Inland Revenue to refund tax				H £_____
Tax deducted from sub-contractors - see your *Contractor's Statement* (form SC35)				I £_____
	C+D	E (1991-92 onwards) C+f (1990-91 or earlier)	C+G	C+H+I
Totals	J £_____·___	J £_____·___	J £_____·___	J £_____
Total SSP recovered/compensation	K £_____·___			
Total SMP recovered/compensation	L £_____·___			
NIC payable to Accounts Office (J minus K minus L)	M £_____			
NIC already paid	N £_____			
NIC now due (M minus N)	O £_____·___			
Tax already paid				P £_____
Tax now due (J minus P)				Q £_____·___

*The current rules for Statutory Sick Pay recovery are in booklet NI268.

** NIC compensation on Statutory Sick Pay due and paid after 5 April 1991 is abolished.

Unit 25: Starting the New Tax Year

25.1 Altering the Tax Details

Firstly, it is necessary to bring the new tax or national insurance details up to date. To do this:

Choose GOVERNMENT PARAMETERS
Choose TAX BANDWIDTHS from the menu

and Enter and alter as follows:

No of bandwidths [2]
Basic Rate Bands [2]

BANDWIDTH		FROM...	TO...	TAX
1	£3000.00	£0.01	£3000.00	20%
2	£20700.00	£3000.00	£23700.00	25%
3	*excess*	£23700.00	*excess*	40%

[Escape] and post.

25.2 Altering the National Insurance Details

Next you should change the National Insurance details:

Choose NI BANDWIDTHS

Alter the limits as follows:

LOWER	£57.00
BAND 1	£100.00
BAND 2	£145.00
BAND 3	£200.00
UPPER	£430.00

[Escape and post]

NI RATES Category [A]

	EMPLOYERS		EMPLOYEES	
	<min>	min	<min>	min
£	%	%	%	%
57 – 99.99	3.60	3.60	2.00	10.00
100 – 144.99	5.60	5.60	2.00	10.00
145 – 199.99	7.60	7.60	2.00	10.00
200 – 430.00	10.20	10.20	2.00	10.00
430 – excess	10.20	10.20	0.00	10.00

25.3 Altering the SSP Rates

To do this:

Choose SSP RATES and enter:

	THRESHOLD	FROM...	TO...	RATE
1	£57.00	£57.00	£199.99	£46.95
2	£200.00	£200.00	*excess*	£52.50

[Escape]

25.4 Altering the SMP Rates

Choose SMP RATES and enter:

LOWER RATE   £47.95
HIGHER RATE   90% of average earnings for first 6 weeks

You are now in a position to enter the April PAYROLL.

Unit 26: Statutory Maternity Pay (SMP)

26.1 Statutory Maternity Pay (SMP)

Any female employee who has been regularly employed in the company for at least 26 weeks and whose earnings are above the lower earnings limit for NI contributions, is entitled to SMP. For all the details of SMP payments you should obtain a copy of the Social Security Guide for Employers as this is a complicated subject.

However, you can find out an example of how the system works by tackling the following situation for Family Favourites.

Maureen O'Mara has been working full time for the company since April 1991.

This means that she has been employed for more than two years and is therefore entitled to the higher rate of SMP, payable for the period of 18 weeks. She has presented the company with a maternity certificate (Form MAT B1), and has correctly given the company at least 21 days notice of her intention to start her maternity leave on 18th April 1994.

You need therefore to set up her records for SMP.

To do this:

> Choose STATUTORY MATERNITY PAY from the menu and enter
> Choose INITIALISE SMP DATES

Enter Maureens Employee number 5 and type in the information as detailed in the following.

Date baby due	26th June 1994
Medical evidence	[Yes] as Form MATB1 8th March 1994
Average weekly wage	Press F3 for this to be calculated automatically and select [yes]. Because the wage records have not been on the computer long enough you will have to calculate this yourself.
	Next month it will be automatic.
	NOTE: to calculate the weekly average multiply the last two monthly payments by 6 and divide by 52.
Employment began	As entered.
Employment ended	15th April 1994.
Minimum hours	36 hour week.
Fair dismissal	Yes.

The bottom part of the screen should now display the SMP calculations for the 18 week period.

Unit 27: Statutory Sick Pay (SSP)

For the full information on SSP you should consult the Social Security Guide for SSP. But as an example of how the system works and how the Payroll II Programme can help you the following exercise for Alan Simms from Family Favourites will act as a guide.

Family Favourites can claim back 80% of the SSP rate paid to an employee. This is done by a deduction from the companies monthly NI payment.

The Sage Payroll Programme automatically calculates the rate for SSP, the qualifying days, the amount of SSP, and the system keeps a diary for each employee.

Before entering any SSP details it is important to check that the GOVERNMENT PARAMETERS are correct for April 1994.

To do this:

Choose	GOVERNMENT PARAMETERS
Choose	SSP PARAMETERS and check the values
Choose	SSP RATES and check the rates

27.1 Initialising SSP

Choose	STATUTORY SICK PAY and enter
Choose	8 WEEKS GROSS PAY
Enter	Employee number 3 Alan Simms.
Enter	Start of the Period Incapable for Work (PIW) 130494

The end of the period would be entered next or, as Alan is still away ill, the month end date.

The type is [A]

You will be asked   [BLOCK FILL :   NO   YES]

Answer 'YES' and the diary will be automatically filled for the dates you have entered.

Unit 28: April 1994 Payroll

28.1 April 1994 Payroll

The details of FAMILY FAVOURITES payroll for April will be the same as March (See Module 2), apart from the following alterations. Alan Simms is away ill from 13th April 1994 and a Doctors note is received to confirm this. On April 15th,

Mrs Maureen OMara leaves the company to have a baby. A new employee, Miss Karen Foster, joins the company on the 11th April 1994. These alterations will enable you to gain experience of statutory sick pay and maternity pay.

Other payroll details for April are as follows:

❏ No bonus is payable in April.

❏ Jonathon Summers and Ghanja Singh both work 9 hours overtime at time and a half.

❏ Ms Marion Brooker receives a rise of £55.00 per month.

To cater for these changes you will firstly need to add Karen to the Payroll.

28.2 Enter a New Employee

To do this:

Choose EMPLOYEE DETAILS
Choose ADD A NEW EMPLOYEE and enter the following..

Karen Foster
9 Amington Avenue
Tamworth
Staffordshire
B79 8FE

Date of Birth 14th May 1972.
Tax code 344L
NI Category A
NI No BB012231A.

[page down]

and enter Karen in the packing department at a salary of £450.00 per month. She will be entitled to a bonus.

[page down]

and enter the BANK DETAILS:

T.S.B. BANK PLC
CHURCH STREET
TAMWORTH
SORT CODE 11-06-92 ACCOUNT NO 12340654
No previous employment details to enter.

28.3 Alter Employees Record

Next you should enter any amendments for the new payroll. By staying in the sub menu you can enter the new wage rate for Marion and the overtime requirements for Jonathon and Ghanja.

Choose AMEND EMPLOYEE RECORDS
Choose TABLE SELECTIONS

Select number 4 and enter Marion's new salary under:

RATES OF PAY   salary £750.00

Next select number 6 and enter Jonathon's overtime by adding a 3 under 2 for Basic Rate.

Work out the time and half rate and enter it under the hourly rate.

Repeat this procedure for Ghanja [number 7].

You can now process the April Payroll.

28.4 Processing the April Payroll

Choose PROCESSING PAYROLL from the Sub-Menu

Refer to Unit 23 if you need help. Make sure you enter the correct payroll date as the 30th April 1994. If you do not clear the payments file you must make sure that you delete the bonus payments from the last month.

All the entries should be straight forward apart from the following:

Employee No. 3 Alan Simms.

Although Alan has only worked for the first 8 days of the month, it is the company policy to make up the SSP to his normal monthly pay.

To do this move the cursor above the payment type and press [F3].

You will be asked if you wish to ADJUST for SSP/SMP; answer YES.

The salary will be automatically adjusted.

Employee No. 5 Maureen O'Mara.

Adjust the monthly salary as Alan's.

Employees No. 6 & 7 Jonathon Summers and Ghanja Singh.

Enter 9 hours overtime for both these employees.

Employee No. 10 Karen Foster.

Karen started work on 11th April 1994 so she has only worked for 15 of the 21 working days in April. Divide 15 by 21 and enter .7143 instead of 1 and the salary will be adjusted accordingly.

You should now check out the monthly payroll by printing out the PAYMENT SUMMARY.

If you are satisfied that this is correct go to UPDATE RECORDS

and complete the months postings by printing out the

GIRO ANALYSIS
PAYSLIPS
PRINT GIROS
COLLECTOR OF TAXES

IAB Examination Paper

Diploma in Computerised Bookkeeping

This section is primarily for students taking the Diploma Examination in Computerised Book-keeping.

The following Assignment is the December 1993 examination the contents of which are covered in Modules 1 to 20.

A list of the Colleges providing this course can be obtained from:
International Association of Book-Keepers.
Burford House, 44 London Road
Sevenoaks, Kent, England
TH13 1AS

International Association of Book-Keepers (I.A.B.)
Diploma in Computerised Book-Keeping using Sage
EXAMINATION ASSIGNMENT 1

Time allowed: 2 Hours

ASSIGNMENT

❏ From the information listed below open up the relevant ledger accounts, including separate sales, purchase and stock accounts for widgets and thrappets. Post the transactions to the ledger and prepare the following reports at the 30th April 1993.

1) Customer statements

2) Print the following after making any month end adjustments:

Audit Trails	Sales and Purchase Day Books
Journals	Account Histories
Trial Balance	Profit and Loss Account
Balance Sheet	

3) Close down the system correctly ensuring correct month end procedure

INFORMATION

❏ ABC Ltd was formed on the 1st April 1993 to take over the partnership from Adam, Brian and Clive. The business sold Widgets and Thrappets. The limited company only took over the fixed assets, stock and the bank balance.

❏ The opening Trial Balance extracted on 1st April 1993 was as follows

	£
Property	200,000
Plant and Equipment	50,000
Office Equipment	10,000
Motor Vehicles	20,000
Stock - Widgets	6,000
Stock - Thrappets	4,000
Bank Account	10,000
Share Capital	300,000

❏ The invoices for the month were as follows

5/4/93 Invoice 10000
    B Davies & Co, St Leonards Way, Kettering, Northants
    Thrappets £2000.00 VAT £350.00 Total £2350.00

10/4/93 Invoice 10001
    C Grant Ltd, New York Road, Newcastle upon Tyne. NE6 4SP

      Widgets £5000 VAT £875 Total £5875

   18/4/93 Invoice 10002

      Egerton & Co, 51 Maxwell Road, Enfield, Middlesex

      Widgets £6000 VAT £1050 Total £7050

   24/4/93 Invoice 10003

      B Davies & Co, St Leonards Way, Kettering, Northants

      Thrappets £1000 VAT £175 Total £1175

   28/4/93 Invoice 10004

      CEL Supplies Ltd, PO Box 100, Birmingham. B1 2QT

      Widgets £500 VAT £87.50 Total £587.50

❏ The following Credit Note was raised

   24/4/93 CN 001

      Egerton & Co 51 Maxwell Road, Enfield, Middlesex

      Allowance for delivery charges paid by customer £200 plus VAT £35

      Total £235.00

❏ The following purchase invoices were received

   10/4/93 Invoice 234567

      Widget Supplies Inc. Great West Road, London W15

      Widgets £6000 VAT £1050

      Total £7050

   12/4/93 Invoice 12987

      C Grant Ltd, New York Road, Newcastle upon Tyne NE 4SP

      Thrappets £1000 VAT £175

      Total £1175

   20/4/93 Invoice 56398

      Southern Stationers Ltd, London Road, Severn Oaks, Kent TN13 4DS.

      Stationery £200.00 VAT 35.00

      Total £235.00

❏ An Analysis of the cheque stubs revealed

  2/4/93   Cheque 100001 for £500 was cashed for petty cash

  14/4/93 Cheque 100002 for £3000 for the rent 1/4/93 to 30/6/93

  20/4/93 Cheque 100003 monthly salaries £2000.

❏ The following receipts had been received

  5/4/93   A cheque for 48,000 had been received for rent of the premises for twelve months.

  20/4/93 A cheque was received for £45,000 plus VAT £7875 for the sale of the plant and equipment from the factory

  30/4/93 Cheque was received from C Grant Ltd in settlement of their account deducting the amount of the invoice due to them.

❏ Petty Cash

  10/4/93 Postage £25.00

  12/4/93 General expenses £23.50 inc VAT

  17/4/93 Petrol £117.50 inc VAT

  27/4/93 Repairs to Motor Car £200 VAT £35.00

❏ On 30th April 1993 £80,000 was transferred to a High Interest Account.

Part 2: Processing accounting information manually and then transferring it to a computerised system

Introduction

You should work through this part in sequence. You will first process the accounting details manually, and then transfer the details to the computerised system, enabling you to compare the two methods. Ensure that you retain your computerised results on disk for subsequent use.

The units in this part of the book (except Unit 7) are designed to fulfil the NVQ accounting requirements, the first four units at Level 2, and the last three at Level 3.

In each unit you will:

❒ work through January transactions manually;

❒ compare your results with the answers in the Appendix;

❒ go to the relevant units in Part 1 to process the same information on the computer.

In some units you will also:

❒ check your computerised results with your manual results;

❒ work through February transactions manually (there are no answers supplied for this month's transactions);

❒ go to the relevant units in Part 1 to process the same information on the computer;

❒ check your computerised results for February against your manual results.

Note. If you are not interested in how a manual system would operate, do not do this part, but work through Part 1.

Contents

Unit I: Recording of sales and purchases

A satisfactory completion of the tasks in this unit could be used for NVQ Level 2 and 20, and Level 3 Element 5.1.

In this unit you will:

☐ Prepare a Purchase and Returns Day Book.

☐ Prepare a Sales and Returns Day Book.

☐ Prepare a Sales and Purchases Ledger.

☐ Calculate a list of Outstanding Debtors and Creditors.

☐ Process units 1 to 8 of Part 1.

☐ Print out a list of Debtors and Creditors.

Activities

Task 1

Draw up a Purchase Day Book and a Returns Outward Book to show Date, Details, Invoice Reference, Amount VAT and Total.

Taking the information from Part 1, Unit 4.2 (page 13), enter the purchase invoices and credit Notes Unit 4.4 (page 22).

Total the amount, VAT and total columns to find the total value of purchases and returns for the month.

Task 2

Prepare ledger accounts for all the suppliers. Rule up the ledger accounts to show debits on left hand side and credits on the right. Enter the opening balances from Unit 3.2 (page 11) on the credit side of the ledger and then the purchase invoices and credit notes as recorded in the day books.

Task 3

Now enter the cheques paid to suppliers (Unit 5.2 page 26).

Next, balance off these supplier's ledger accounts and carry down the balances to February.

Finally, prepare a list of Creditors (Supplier's Accounts) showing the amounts outstanding.

Task 4

Prepare a Sales Day Book and a Returns Inwards Book and line them up to show the same details as required in task 1.

From Part 1, enter the Sales Invoices and Credit Notes Unit 4.3 pages 18 and Unit 4.4 page 22.

Total the columns to show the months sales on credit and the customer returns and the VAT.

Task 5

As task 2, make out Ledger Accounts for every customer and enter the opening balances as debits (from Unit 3.1 page 10) on the left hand side.

Next enter the cheques received from customers (Unit 5.1 page 24), and then check the bank statement (Unit 7 page 30) to see if any direct receipts have been made (i.e. giros).

Finally, prepare a list of debtors (customers) showing the amounts outstanding, analysed by months.

Task 6

Go to Part 1 and process Getting Started and Units 1, 2, 3, 4 and 5, and then produce the necessary printouts to compare with your manual records. Your records should also be compared with the suggested solutions in the Appendix.

Task 7

After completion of these tasks you can repeat the same activities with the February transactions as contained in Part 1, Units 14–18. You may need some help from your tutor with this task as no solutions are given.

Task 8

Finally, you need to present a file containing tasks 1–7. [A brief introduction to this presentation should explain the reasons for these activities.

Some things to bear in mind when compiling your file:

- ☐ Be as neat as possible.
- ☐ Make sure your day books add across and down.
- ☐ Find out how to balance off your Ledger Accounts and bring the balances down.
- ☐ Do your manual records compare with your Computer Produced reports?
- ☐ When you have completed all the activities number all the pages and include a contents page.

Unit II: Cash books and bank reconciliation

A satisfactory completion of all the tasks in this unit could be used for NVQ Level 2, Units 1 and 20, and Level 3 Element 5.1.

In this Unit you will:

- ☐ Prepare a Cash Book Showing receipts and payments.
- ☐ Calculate the Cash Book balance at the month end.
- ☐ Reconcile the Cash Book balance to the Bank Balance.
- ☐ Prepare a Petty Cash Book.
- ☐ Calculate the Petty Cash Balance and build up the float.

☐ Process Units 5–7 on the computer from Part 1 and produce a print out of the Bank Control Account to compare with your records

☐ Process Unit 6 and print out the Petty Cash Control Account to compare with your Petty Cash Book.

☐ Complete the same activities for the February transactions, Units 17–8.

Activities

Task 1

Prepare a Cash Book (see following page for a sample) and enter the Cheques contained in Part 1 (Units 5 to 7). Make sure that the full details of each payment is included,

The opening balance should be taken from the Trial Balance (Unit 3.3 page 12).

Task 2

After all these entries have been recorded tick them off against the Bank Statement for January (Unit 7).

Bring the Cash Book up to date by entering items from the Bank Statement which have not been recorded, (i.e. bank charges, interest or standing orders etc).

Add up the Cash Book columns to show the balance at the month end.

Task 3

Compare the opening Cash Book and Bank Statement balances and investigate any differences.

Agree the Cash Book balance to the Bank Statement balance, by preparing a Reconciliation Statement at the 31st January. Always start with the Cash Book balance and add any payments not entered on the Bank Statement and deduct any receipts not entered on the Bank Statement.

Task 4

Draw up a Petty Cash Book (see page 104 for sample) and enter all the details from Unit 6. Make sure the date details and Folio number are included. The details should be entered showing separate totals for the various expenses and VAT.

Total the Petty Cash Book for the month and restore the closing balance to the required float.

Task 5

Compare your results with the solutions contained in the rear of the book.

Then use the computer to process Units 5–7 of Part 1 and produce the required print outs for comparison with your Cash Book and Petty Cash Book.

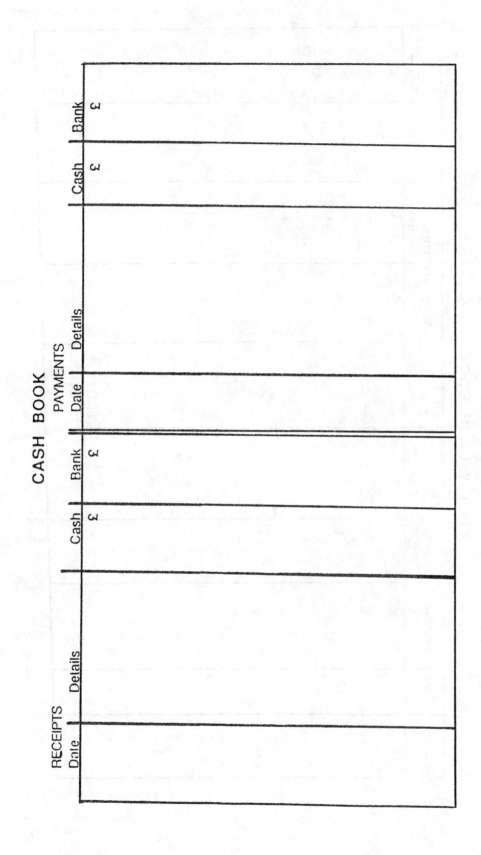

PETTY CASH BOOK

Receipts	Date	Details	Voucher No.	Total Payment	Analysis columns				
£				£	Postages	Travel	Stationery	Meals	VAT
					£	£	£	£	£

Task 6

You can now attempt the same activities for the month of February by processing Units 17 and 18 of Part 1.

Reconcile your Bank and Cash Books and compare the results with the computer figures you produce

Task 7

Finally, you need to present a file containing Tasks 1 to 7.

A brief introduction to your presentation should explain what you have done, and why.

Some things to bear in mind when compiling your file:

- ❐ Be as neat as you can.
- ❐ Make sure sufficient detail is included to enable the tracing and auditing of documents.
- ❐ Check all balances and calculations.
- ❐ Do the computer reports agree with the reports you have made?
- ❐ When you have finished number all the pages and draw up a Contents Page.

Unit III: Calculation of wages, personal tax and National Insurance deductions

A satisfactory completion of this Unit could be used for activities for NVQ Level 2, Units 3 and 20, and Level 3 Element 5.1.

In this unit you will:

- ❐ Prepare the monthly payroll.
- ❐ Calculate the gross wages and salaries.
- ❐ Work out the required deductions for tax and NI.
- ❐ Calculate the net wages.
- ❐ Prepare a wage slip for each employee to clearly show the gross wage and the deductions.
- ❐ Make up the P11 Forms up to date and complete the year end tax figures.
- ❐ Process the same information on the computer using Units 21, 22, 23 and 24 and print out the payroll and the wage slips.
- ❐ Print out the P11 deduction forms and the year end P35 summary and P60 certificates.

```
MONTHLY PAYROLL MARCH 1994

NAME                   TAX CODE  NI CAT.  RATE              BONUS

Mr Roger Brian Sims      525H       A     £712pm            £350
Mrs Barbara Sunter       344L       A     100Hrs at £2.50   10%
Mr Alan Simms            79L        A     £650pm            10%
Ms Marion Brooker        344L       A     £695pm            10%
Mrs Maureen OMara        344L       A     £480pm            10%
Mr Jonathon Summers      344L       A     120Hrs at £2.65   10%
Mr Ghanja Singh          344L       A     140Hrs at £2.95   10%
Mr Benjamin Sykes        344L       A     140Hrs at £3.20   10%
Ms Paula Ann Browne      344L       A     65Hrs at £2.75    10%
```

Activities

Task 1

Prepare an analysis sheet in the format of a wages book to show the following details: Name, Taxcode, Gross pay this month, Bonus, Add Pay to date, Total Gross Pay to date, Free Pay, Taxable Pay, Tax to date, Less tax paid, Tax this month, Employee's National Insurance, Pension, Total deductions, Net pay, Employers National Insurance.

Using the above information enter the employees names and work out the gross wage for each individual.

Total the gross wages for the month.

Next, using the P11 deduction sheet extracts, at the rear of this unit, enter the pay to date and calculate the new total pay to date.

Add these totals for the month and ensure they cross cast.

Task 2

Turn to Table A, Pay Adjustment Tables for Month 12, at the rear of this unit and enter the total free pay to date using the employees tax code for each case.

Deduct the Free Pay from the Total Pay to Date to calculate the Taxable Pay and check your figures by cross casting the totals.

The Tax for this period is calculated by comparing the Taxable pay to Table B, Subtration tables, at the end of this unit.

To find the tax to deduct for this month enter the employees Brought Forward tax from the P11 sheets and deduct it from the tax for this month.

Add the columns across and down to make sure your figures are correct.

Task 3

Enter the National Insurance for the month by reference to the Monthly Table A.

Make sure you enter the employees' figures in the wage analysis calculation and the employer's figures separately.

Add the Tax, National Insurance and Pension to find the total deductions, and then calculate the Net pay for the month.

Bring the P11 sheets up to date by entering the above information. Complete the P11 sheets for the year to 31st March 1994 and prepare the Year End Company Tax Return, P35 Form, after the P11 Sheets.

Task 4

Compare your figures with the suggested solutions and then use the computer to process Units 21 to 24 of Part 1 and then produce the necessary print-outs to compare with your manual records.

Task 5

Finally. you need to present a file containing all the activities you have completed in this Unit.

A brief introduction to this presentation should contain an explanation and some comments or observations for the activities you have completed.

Some things to bear in mind when compiling your file:

❑ Be as neat as possible and line up your figures to make additions and calculations easier.

❑ Make sure the columns of your Wages Book add across and down.

❑ Try and compare your analysis records with a proper wages book and, if you wish, alter your records in whatever way you require to make it as clear as possible.

❑ Do your manual records compare with the Computer Produced Reports? If not, briefly explain why you think this is not so.

❑ When you have completed all the required activities, number all the pages and include a contents page.

TABLE A - PAY ADJUSTMENT   Month 12
Mar 6 to Apr 5

Code	Total pay adjustment to date £	Code	Total pay adjustment to date £	Code	Total pay adjustment to date £	Code	Total pay adjustment to date £	Code	Total pay adjustment to date £	Code	Total pay adjustment to date £	Code	Total pay adjustment to date £	Code	Total pay adjustment to date £	Code	Total pay adjustment to date £
0	NIL																
1	19.08	61	619.08	121	1219.08	181	1819.08	241	2419.08	301	3019.08	351	3519.00	401	4019.04	451	4519.08
2	29.04	62	629.04	122	1229.04	182	1829.04	242	2429.04	302	3029.04	352	3529.08	402	4029.00	452	4529.04
3	39.00	63	639.00	123	1239.00	183	1839.00	243	2439.00	303	3039.00	353	3539.04	403	4039.08	453	4539.00
4	49.08	64	649.08	124	1249.08	184	1849.08	244	2449.08	304	3049.08	354	3549.00	404	4049.04	454	4549.08
5	59.04	65	659.04	125	1259.04	185	1859.04	245	2459.04	305	3059.04	355	3559.08	405	4059.00	455	4559.04
6	69.00	66	669.00	126	1269.00	186	1869.00	246	2469.00	306	3069.00	356	3569.04	406	4069.08	456	4569.00
7	79.08	67	679.08	127	1279.08	187	1879.08	247	2479.08	307	3079.08	357	3579.00	407	4079.04	457	4579.08
8	89.04	68	689.04	128	1289.04	188	1889.04	248	2489.04	308	3089.04	358	3589.08	408	4089.00	458	4589.04
9	99.00	69	699.00	129	1299.00	189	1899.00	249	2499.00	309	3099.00	359	3599.04	409	4099.08	459	4599.00
10	109.08	70	709.08	130	1309.08	190	1909.08	250	2509.08	310	3109.08	360	3609.00	410	4109.04	460	4609.08
11	119.04	71	719.04	131	1319.04	191	1919.04	251	2519.04	311	3119.04	361	3619.08	411	4119.00	461	4619.04
12	129.00	72	729.00	132	1329.00	192	1929.00	252	2529.00	312	3129.00	362	3629.04	412	4129.08	462	4629.00
13	139.08	73	739.08	133	1339.08	193	1939.08	253	2539.08	313	3139.08	363	3639.00	413	4139.04	463	4639.08
14	149.04	74	749.04	134	1349.04	194	1949.04	254	2549.04	314	3149.04	364	3649.08	414	4149.00	464	4649.04
15	159.00	75	759.00	135	1359.00	195	1959.00	255	2559.00	315	3159.00	365	3659.04	415	4159.08	465	4659.00
16	169.08	76	769.08	136	1369.08	196	1969.08	256	2569.08	316	3169.08	366	3669.00	416	4169.04	466	4669.08
17	179.04	77	779.04	137	1379.04	197	1979.04	257	2579.04	317	3179.04	367	3679.08	417	4179.00	467	4679.04
18	189.00	78	789.00	138	1389.00	198	1989.00	258	2589.00	318	3189.00	368	3689.04	418	4189.08	468	4689.00
19	199.08	79	799.08	139	1399.08	199	1999.08	259	2599.08	319	3199.08	369	3699.00	419	4199.04	469	4699.08
20	209.04	80	809.04	140	1409.04	200	2009.04	260	2609.04	320	3209.04	370	3709.08	420	4209.00	470	4709.04
21	219.00	81	819.00	141	1419.00	201	2019.00	261	2619.00	321	3219.00	371	3719.04	421	4219.08	471	4719.00
22	229.08	82	829.08	142	1429.08	202	2029.08	262	2629.08	322	3229.08	372	3729.00	422	4229.04	472	4729.08
23	239.04	83	839.04	143	1439.04	203	2039.04	263	2639.04	323	3239.04	373	3739.08	423	4239.00	473	4739.04
24	249.00	84	849.00	144	1449.00	204	2049.00	264	2649.00	324	3249.00	374	3749.04	424	4249.08	474	4749.00
25	259.08	85	859.08	145	1459.08	205	2059.08	265	2659.08	325	3259.08	375	3759.00	425	4259.04	475	4759.08
26	269.04	86	869.04	146	1469.04	206	2069.04	266	2669.04	326	3269.04	376	3769.08	426	4269.00	476	4769.04
27	279.00	87	879.00	147	1479.00	207	2079.00	267	2679.00	327	3279.00	377	3779.04	427	4279.08	477	4779.00
28	289.08	88	889.08	148	1489.08	208	2089.08	268	2689.08	328	3289.08	378	3789.00	428	4289.04	478	4789.08
29	299.04	89	899.04	149	1499.04	209	2099.04	269	2699.04	329	3299.04	379	3799.08	429	4299.00	479	4799.04
30	309.00	90	909.00	150	1509.00	210	2109.00	270	2709.00	330	3309.00	380	3809.04	430	4309.08	480	4809.00
31	319.08	91	919.08	151	1519.08	211	2119.08	271	2719.08	331	3319.08	381	3819.00	431	4319.04	481	4819.08
32	329.04	92	929.04	152	1529.04	212	2129.04	272	2729.04	332	3329.04	382	3829.08	432	4329.00	482	4829.04
33	339.00	93	939.00	153	1539.00	213	2139.00	273	2739.00	333	3339.00	383	3839.04	433	4339.08	483	4839.00
34	349.08	94	949.08	154	1549.08	214	2149.08	274	2749.08	334	3349.08	384	3849.00	434	4349.04	484	4849.08
35	359.04	95	959.04	155	1559.04	215	2159.04	275	2759.04	335	3359.04	385	3859.08	435	4359.00	485	4859.04
36	369.00	96	969.00	156	1569.00	216	2169.00	276	2769.00	336	3369.00	386	3869.04	436	4369.08	486	4869.00
37	379.08	97	979.08	157	1579.08	217	2179.08	277	2779.08	337	3379.08	387	3879.00	437	4379.04	487	4879.08
38	389.04	98	989.04	158	1589.04	218	2189.04	278	2789.04	338	3389.04	388	3889.08	438	4389.00	488	4889.04
39	399.00	99	999.00	159	1599.00	219	2199.00	279	2799.00	339	3399.00	389	3899.04	439	4399.08	489	4899.00
40	409.08	100	1009.08	160	1609.08	220	2209.08	280	2809.08	340	3409.08	390	3909.00	440	4409.04	490	4909.08
41	419.04	101	1019.04	161	1619.04	221	2219.04	281	2819.04	341	3419.04	391	3919.08	441	4419.00	491	4919.04
42	429.00	102	1029.00	162	1629.00	222	2229.00	282	2829.00	342	3429.00	392	3929.04	442	4429.08	492	4929.00
43	439.08	103	1039.08	163	1639.08	223	2239.08	283	2839.08	343	3439.08	393	3939.00	443	4439.04	493	4939.08
44	449.04	104	1049.04	164	1649.04	224	2249.04	284	2849.04	344	3449.04	394	3949.08	444	4449.00	494	4949.04
45	459.00	105	1059.00	165	1659.00	225	2259.00	285	2859.00	345	3459.00	395	3959.04	445	4459.08	495	4959.00
46	469.08	106	1069.08	166	1669.08	226	2269.08	286	2869.08	346	3469.08	396	3969.00	446	4469.04	496	4969.08
47	479.04	107	1079.04	167	1679.04	227	2279.04	287	2879.04	347	3479.04	397	3979.08	447	4479.00	497	4979.04
48	489.00	108	1089.00	168	1689.00	228	2289.00	288	2889.00	348	3489.00	398	3989.04	448	4489.08	498	4989.00
49	499.08	109	1099.08	169	1699.08	229	2299.08	289	2899.08	349	3499.08	399	3999.00	449	4499.04	499	4999.08
50	509.04	110	1109.04	170	1709.04	230	2309.04	290	2909.04	350	3509.04	400	4009.08	450	4509.00	500	5009.04
51	519.00	111	1119.00	171	1719.00	231	2319.00	291	2919.00								
52	529.08	112	1129.08	172	1729.08	232	2329.08	292	2929.08								
53	539.04	113	1139.04	173	1739.04	233	2339.04	293	2939.04								
54	549.00	114	1149.00	174	1749.00	234	2349.00	294	2949.00								
55	559.08	115	1159.08	175	1759.08	235	2359.08	295	2959.08								
56	569.04	116	1169.04	176	1769.04	236	2369.04	296	2969.04								
57	579.00	117	1179.00	177	1779.00	237	2379.00	297	2979.00								
58	589.08	118	1189.08	178	1789.08	238	2389.08	298	2989.08								
59	599.04	119	1199.04	179	1799.04	239	2399.04	299	2999.04								
60	609.00	120	1209.00	180	1809.00	240	2409.00	300	3009.00								

Pay adjustment where code exceeds 500

1. Where the code is in the range **501** to **1000** inclusive proceed as follows:

   a. Subtract **500** from the code and use the balance of the code to obtain a pay adjustment figure from the table above.

   b. Add this pay adjustment figure to the figure given in the box alongside to obtain the figure of total pay adjustment to date   * | 5000.04 |

2. Where the code **exceeds 1000** follow the instructions on **page 2**.

Printed in the UK for HMSO 2/93. MAP 0102091. C17000. 22993.

Table B
(Tax at 25%)

Pages 2 and 3 tell you when to use these tables

Remember to use the Subtraction Tables on Page 7

Tax Due on Taxable Pay from £1 to £99

Total TAXABLE PAY to date	Total TAX DUE to date	Total TAXABLE PAY to date	Total TAX DUE to date
£	£	£	£
1	0.25	61	15.25
2	0.50	62	15.50
3	0.75	63	15.75
4	1.00	64	16.00
5	1.25	65	16.25
6	1.50	66	16.50
7	1.75	67	16.75
8	2.00	68	17.00
9	2.25	69	17.25
10	2.50	70	17.50
11	2.75	71	17.75
12	3.00	72	18.00
13	3.25	73	18.25
14	3.50	74	18.50
15	3.75	75	18.75
16	4.00	76	19.00
17	4.25	77	19.25
18	4.50	78	19.50
19	4.75	79	19.75
20	5.00	80	20.00
21	5.25	81	20.25
22	5.50	82	20.50
23	5.75	83	20.75
24	6.00	84	21.00
25	6.25	85	21.25
26	6.50	86	21.50
27	6.75	87	21.75
28	7.00	88	22.00
29	7.25	89	22.25
30	7.50	90	22.50
31	7.75	91	22.75
32	8.00	92	23.00
33	8.25	93	23.25
34	8.50	94	23.50
35	8.75	95	23.75
36	9.00	96	24.00
37	9.25	97	24.25
38	9.50	98	24.50
39	9.75	99	24.75
40	10.00		
41	10.25		
42	10.50		
43	10.75		
44	11.00		
45	11.25		
46	11.50		
47	11.75		
48	12.00		
49	12.25		
50	12.50		
51	12.75		
52	13.00		
53	13.25		
54	13.50		
55	13.75		
56	14.00		
57	14.25		
58	14.50		
59	14.75		
60	15.00		

Tax Due on Taxable Pay from £100 to £23,700

Total TAXABLE PAY to date	Total TAX DUE to date	Total TAXABLE PAY to date	Total TAX DUE to date	Total TAXABLE PAY to date	Total TAX DUE to date	Total TAXABLE PAY to date	Total TAX DUE to date
£	£	£	£	£	£	£	£
100	25.00	6100	1525.00	12100	3025.00	18100	4525.00
200	50.00	6200	1550.00	12200	3050.00	18200	4550.00
300	75.00	6300	1575.00	12300	3075.00	18300	4575.00
400	100.00	6400	1600.00	12400	3100.00	18400	4600.00
500	125.00	6500	1625.00	12500	3125.00	18500	4625.00
600	150.00	6600	1650.00	12600	3150.00	18600	4650.00
700	175.00	6700	1675.00	12700	3175.00	18700	4675.00
800	200.00	6800	1700.00	12800	3200.00	18800	4700.00
900	225.00	6900	1725.00	12900	3225.00	18900	4725.00
1000	250.00	7000	1750.00	13000	3250.00	19000	4750.00
1100	275.00	7100	1775.00	13100	3275.00	19100	4775.00
1200	300.00	7200	1800.00	13200	3300.00	19200	4800.00
1300	325.00	7300	1825.00	13300	3325.00	19300	4825.00
1400	350.00	7400	1850.00	13400	3350.00	19400	4850.00
1500	375.00	7500	1875.00	13500	3375.00	19500	4875.00
1600	400.00	7600	1900.00	13600	3400.00	19600	4900.00
1700	425.00	7700	1925.00	13700	3425.00	19700	4925.00
1800	450.00	7800	1950.00	13800	3450.00	19800	4950.00
1900	475.00	7900	1975.00	13900	3475.00	19900	4975.00
2000	500.00	8000	2000.00	14000	3500.00	20000	5000.00
2100	525.00	8100	2025.00	14100	3525.00	20100	5025.00
2200	550.00	8200	2050.00	14200	3550.00	20200	5050.00
2300	575.00	8300	2075.00	14300	3575.00	20300	5075.00
2400	600.00	8400	2100.00	14400	3600.00	20400	5100.00
2500	625.00	8500	2125.00	14500	3625.00	20500	5125.00
2600	650.00	8600	2150.00	14600	3650.00	20600	5150.00
2700	675.00	8700	2175.00	14700	3675.00	20700	5175.00
2800	700.00	8800	2200.00	14800	3700.00	20800	5200.00
2900	725.00	8900	2225.00	14900	3725.00	20900	5225.00
3000	750.00	9000	2250.00	15000	3750.00	21000	5250.00
3100	775.00	9100	2275.00	15100	3775.00	21100	5275.00
3200	800.00	9200	2300.00	15200	3800.00	21200	5300.00
3300	825.00	9300	2325.00	15300	3825.00	21300	5325.00
3400	850.00	9400	2350.00	15400	3850.00	21400	5350.00
3500	875.00	9500	2375.00	15500	3875.00	21500	5375.00
3600	900.00	9600	2400.00	15600	3900.00	21600	5400.00
3700	925.00	9700	2425.00	15700	3925.00	21700	5425.00
3800	950.00	9800	2450.00	15800	3950.00	21800	5450.00
3900	975.00	9900	2475.00	15900	3975.00	21900	5475.00
4000	1000.00	10000	2500.00	16000	4000.00	22000	5500.00
4100	1025.00	10100	2525.00	16100	4025.00	22100	5525.00
4200	1050.00	10200	2550.00	16200	4050.00	22200	5550.00
4300	1075.00	10300	2575.00	16300	4075.00	22300	5575.00
4400	1100.00	10400	2600.00	16400	4100.00	22400	5600.00
4500	1125.00	10500	2625.00	16500	4125.00	22500	5625.00
4600	1150.00	10600	2650.00	16600	4150.00	22600	5650.00
4700	1175.00	10700	2675.00	16700	4175.00	22700	5675.00
4800	1200.00	10800	2700.00	16800	4200.00	22800	5700.00
4900	1225.00	10900	2725.00	16900	4225.00	22900	5725.00
5000	1250.00	11000	2750.00	17000	4250.00	23000	5750.00
5100	1275.00	11100	2775.00	17100	4275.00	23100	5775.00
5200	1300.00	11200	2800.00	17200	4300.00	23200	5800.00
5300	1325.00	11300	2825.00	17300	4325.00	23300	5825.00
5400	1350.00	11400	2850.00	17400	4350.00	23400	5850.00
5500	1375.00	11500	2875.00	17500	4375.00	23500	5875.00
5600	1400.00	11600	2900.00	17600	4400.00	23600	5900.00
5700	1425.00	11700	2925.00	17700	4425.00	23700	5925.00
5800	1450.00	11800	2950.00	17800	4450.00		
5900	1475.00	11900	2975.00	17900	4475.00		
6000	1500.00	12000	3000.00	18000	4500.00		

Where the exact amount of taxable pay is not shown, add together the figures for two (or more) entries to make up the amount of taxable pay to the nearest £1 below.

6

Table B Subtraction Tables
(Lower Rate Relief)

Do not use the subtraction tables for code BR

For all ordinary suffix codes and prefix K codes - When you have used the table on Page 6 to work out the tax at 25% refer to the tables below to give the benefit of the lower rate band. Find the week or month in which the pay day falls (it is the same week or month you have used in Tables A) and **subtract** the amount shown to arrive at the tax due.

There is an example below and further examples on Page 8

Employee paid at Weekly rates

Week No.	Amount to subtract £
1	2.41
2	4.81
3	7.22
4	9.62
5	12.02
6	14.43
7	16.83
8	19.24
9	21.64
10	24.04
11	26.45
12	28.85
13	31.25
14	33.66
15	36.06
16	38.47
17	40.87
18	43.27
19	45.68
20	48.08
21	50.49
22	52.89
23	55.29
24	57.70
25	60.10
26	62.50
27	64.91
28	67.31
29	69.72
30	72.12
31	74.52
32	76.93
33	79.33
34	81.74
35	84.14
36	86.54
37	88.95
38	91.35
39	93.75
40	96.16
41	98.56
42	100.97
43	103.37
44	105.77
45	108.18
46	110.58
47	112.99
48	115.39
49	117.79
50	120.20
51	122.60
52	125.00

Employee paid at Monthly rates

Month No.	Amount to subtract
1	10.42
2	20.84
3	31.25
4	41.67
5	52.09
6	62.50
7	72.92
8	83.34
9	93.75
10	104.17
11	114.59
12	125.00

Use of Table B   *Example 1*

Employee's code is **344L**
The payment is made in **Week 7**

Pay in the week	£ 200
Previous pay to date	£1200
Total pay to date	£1400
Less free pay in Week 7 (from Table A)	£ 464.31
Total taxable pay to date	**£ 935.69**

The tax is worked out by first looking in Table B on Page 6 for the nearest round figure below £935

		Tax due
It is	£900	£225.00
Look in the shaded columns for the remainder	£ 35	£ 8.75
Totals	£935	£233.75

Then give the Lower Rate Relief by looking in the table on this page for Week 7 and subtract the amount from the tax due. It is

£ 16.83

Total tax due to date   **£216.92**

Monthly

**6 April 1993
to 5 April 1994**

Not contracted-out standard rate NI contributions

Before using this table enter "A" in the space provided on the Deductions Working Sheet P11 or substitute (see Instructions).

Use this table
- for employees who are over age 16 and under pension age (65 men, 60 women).
- for employees who have an appropriate personal pension (from 1 July 1988).

Do not use this table
- for married women and widows who pay NI contributions at the reduced rate — see Table B.
- for employees over pension age or for whom form RD950 is held — see Table C.

Entries to be made on P11
- copy the figures from columns 1a, 1b and 1c to columns 1a, 1b and 1c of the P11.

If the exact gross pay is not shown in the table, use the next smaller figure shown.

Earnings on which employee's contributions payable 1a	Total of employee's and employer's contributions payable 1b	Employee's contributions payable 1c	Employer's contributions*	Earnings on which employee's contributions payable 1a	Total of employee's and employer's contributions payable 1b	Employee's contributions payable 1c	Employer's contributions*
£	£	£	£	£	£	£	£
243	16·04	4·86	11·18	403	38·07	19·44	18·63
247	16·85	5·40	11·45	407	38·61	19·80	18·81
251	17·40	5·76	11·64	411	38·95	20·02	18·93
255	17·94	6·12	11·82	412	47·49	20·20	27·29
259	18·49	6·48	12·01	415	48·04	20·52	27·52
263	19·03	6·84	12·19	419	48·67	20·88	27·79
267	19·57	7·20	12·37	423	49·29	21·24	28·05
271	20·12	7·56	12·56	427	49·91	21·60	28·31
275	20·66	7·92	12·74	431	50·54	21·96	28·58
279	21·21	8·28	12·93	435	51·16	22·32	28·84
283	21·75	8·64	13·11	439	51·79	22·68	29·11
287	22·29	9·00	13·29	443	52·41	23·04	29·37
291	22·84	9·36	13·48	447	53·03	23·40	29·63
295	23·38	9·72	13·66	451	53·66	23·76	29·90
299	23·93	10·08	13·85	455	54·28	24·12	30·16
303	24·47	10·44	14·03	459	54·91	24·48	30·43
307	25·01	10·80	14·21	463	55·53	24·84	30·69
311	25·56	11·16	14·40	467	56·15	25·20	30·95
315	26·10	11·52	14·58	471	56·78	25·56	31·22
319	26·65	11·88	14·77	475	57·40	25·92	31·48
323	27·19	12·24	14·95	479	58·03	26·28	31·75
327	27·73	12·60	15·13	483	58·65	26·64	32·01
331	28·28	12·96	15·32	487	59·27	27·00	32·27
335	28·82	13·32	15·50	491	59·90	27·36	32·54
339	29·37	13·68	15·69	495	60·52	27·72	32·80
343	29·91	14·04	15·87	499	61·15	28·08	33·07
347	30·45	14·40	16·05	503	61·77	28·44	33·33
351	31·00	14·76	16·24	507	62·39	28·80	33·59
355	31·54	15·12	16·42	511	63·02	29·16	33·86
359	32·09	15·48	16·61	515	63·64	29·52	34·12
363	32·63	15·84	16·79	519	64·27	29·88	34·39
367	33·17	16·20	16·97	523	64·89	30·24	34·65
371	33·72	16·56	17·16	527	65·51	30·60	34·91
375	34·26	16·92	17·34	531	66·14	30·96	35·18
379	34·81	17·28	17·53	535	66·76	31·32	35·44
383	35·35	17·64	17·71	539	67·39	31·68	35·71
387	35·89	18·00	17·89	543	68·01	32·04	35·97
391	36·44	18·36	18·08	547	68·63	32·40	36·23
395	36·98	18·72	18·26	551	69·26	32·76	36·50
399	37·53	19·08	18·45	555	69·88	33·12	36·76

* for information only — Do not enter on P11

12

Monthly Table A continued
6 April 1993 to 5 April 1994

Earnings on which employee's contributions payable 1a	Total of employee's and employer's contributions payable 1b	Employee's contributions payable 1c	Employer's contributions*
£	£	£	£
559	70·51	33·48	37·03
563	71·13	33·84	37·29
567	71·75	34·20	37·55
571	72·38	34·56	37·82
575	73·00	34·92	38·08
579	73·63	35·28	38·35
583	74·25	35·64	38·61
587	74·87	36·00	38·87
591	75·50	36·36	39·14
595	76·12	36·72	39·40
599	76·75	37·08	39·67
603	77·37	37·44	39·93
607	90·17	37·80	52·37
611	90·88	38·16	52·72
615	91·58	38·52	53·06
619	92·29	38·88	53·41
623	92·99	39·24	53·75
627	93·69	39·60	54·09
631	94·40	39·96	54·44
635	95·10	40·32	54·78
639	95·81	40·68	55·13
643	96·51	41·04	55·47
647	97·21	41·40	55·81
651	97·92	41·76	56·16
655	98·62	42·12	56·50
659	99·33	42·48	56·85
663	100·03	42·84	57·19
667	100·73	43·20	57·53
671	101·44	43·56	57·88
675	102·14	43·92	58·22
679	102·85	44·28	58·57
683	103·55	44·64	58·91
687	104·25	45·00	59·25
691	104·96	45·36	59·60
695	105·66	45·72	59·94
699	106·37	46·08	60·29
703	107·07	46·44	60·63
707	107·77	46·80	60·97
711	108·48	47·16	61·32
715	109·18	47·52	61·66
719	109·89	47·88	62·01
723	110·59	48·24	62·35
727	111·29	48·60	62·69
731	112·00	48·96	63·04
735	112·70	49·32	63·38
739	113·41	49·68	63·73
743	114·11	50·04	64·07
747	114·81	50·40	64·41
751	115·52	50·76	64·76
755	116·22	51·12	65·10
759	116·93	51·48	65·45
763	117·63	51·84	65·79
767	118·33	52·20	66·13
771	119·04	52·56	66·48
775	119·74	52·92	66·82
779	120·45	53·28	67·17
783	121·15	53·64	67·51
787	121·85	54·00	67·85
791	122·56	54·36	68·20
795	123·26	54·72	68·54

Earnings on which employee's contributions payable 1a	Total of employee's and employer's contributions payable 1b	Employee's contributions payable 1c	Employer's contributions*
£	£	£	£
799	123·97	55·08	68·89
803	124·67	55·44	69·23
807	125·37	55·80	69·57
811	126·08	56·16	69·92
815	126·78	56·52	70·26
819	127·49	56·88	70·61
823	128·19	57·24	70·95
827	128·89	57·60	71·29
831	129·60	57·96	71·64
835	130·30	58·32	71·98
839	131·01	58·68	72·33
843	131·53	58·95	72·58
845	147·11	59·13	87·98
847	147·70	59·40	88·30
851	148·47	59·76	88·71
855	149·25	60·12	89·13
859	150·02	60·48	89·54
863	150·80	60·84	89·96
867	151·58	61·20	90·38
871	152·35	61·56	90·79
875	153·13	61·92	91·21
879	153·90	62·28	91·62
883	154·68	62·64	92·04
887	155·46	63·00	92·46
891	156·23	63·36	92·87
895	157·01	63·72	93·29
899	157·78	64·08	93·70
903	158·56	64·44	94·12
907	159·34	64·80	94·54
911	160·11	65·16	94·95
915	160·89	65·52	95·37
919	161·66	65·88	95·78
923	162·44	66·24	96·20
927	163·22	66·60	96·62
931	163·99	66·96	97·03
935	164·77	67·32	97·45
939	165·54	67·68	97·86
943	166·32	68·04	98·28
947	167·10	68·40	98·70
951	167·87	68·76	99·11
955	168·65	69·12	99·53
959	169·42	69·48	99·94
963	170·20	69·84	100·36
967	170·98	70·20	100·78
971	171·75	70·56	101·19
975	172·53	70·92	101·61
979	173·30	71·28	102·02
983	174·08	71·64	102·44
987	174·86	72·00	102·86
991	175·63	72·36	103·27
995	176·41	72·72	103·69
999	177·18	73·08	104·10
1003	177·96	73·44	104·52
1007	178·74	73·80	104·94
1011	179·51	74·16	105·35
1015	180·29	74·52	105·77
1019	181·06	74·88	106·18
1023	181·84	75·24	106·60
1027	182·62	75·60	107·02
1031	183·39	75·96	107·43

* for information only — Do not enter on P11

13

Monthly **Table A** continued
6 April 1993 to 5 April 1994

Earnings on which employee's contributions payable 1a	Total of employee's and employer's contributions payable 1b	Employee's contributions payable 1c	Employer's contributions*		Earnings on which employee's contributions payable 1a	Total of employee's and employer's contributions payable 1b	Employee's contributions payable 1c	Employer's contributions*
£	£	£	£		£	£	£	£
1035	184·17	76·32	107·85		1275	230·73	97·92	132·81
1039	184·94	76·68	108·26		1279	231·50	98·28	133·22
1043	185·72	77·04	108·68		1283	232·28	98·64	133·64
1047	186·50	77·40	109·10		1287	233·06	99·00	134·06
1051	187·27	77·76	109·51		1291	233·83	99·36	134·47
1055	188·05	78·12	109·93		1295	234·61	99·72	134·89
1059	188·82	78·48	110·34		1299	235·38	100·08	135·30
1063	189·60	78·84	110·76		1303	236·16	100·44	135·72
1067	190·38	79·20	111·18		1307	236·94	100·80	136·14
1071	191·15	79·56	111·59		1311	237·71	101·16	136·55
1075	191·93	79·92	112·01		1315	238·49	101·52	136·97
1079	192·70	80·28	112·42		1319	239·26	101·88	137·38
1083	193·48	80·64	112·84		1323	240·04	102·24	137·80
1087	194·26	81·00	113·26		1327	240·82	102·60	138·22
1091	195·03	81·36	113·67		1331	241·59	102·96	138·63
1095	195·81	81·72	114·09		1335	242·37	103·32	139·05
1099	196·58	82·08	114·50		1339	243·14	103·68	139·46
1103	197·36	82·44	114·92		1343	243·92	104·04	139·88
1107	198·14	82·80	115·34		1347	244·70	104·40	140·30
1111	198·91	83·16	115·75		1351	245·47	104·76	140·71
1115	199·69	83·52	116·17		1355	246·25	105·12	141·13
1119	200·46	83·88	116·58		1359	247·02	105·48	141·54
1123	201·24	84·24	117·00		1363	247·80	105·84	141·96
1127	202·02	84·60	117·42		1367	248·58	106·20	142·38
1131	202·79	84·96	117·83		1371	249·35	106·56	142·79
1135	203·57	85·32	118·25		1375	250·13	106·92	143·21
1139	204·34	85·68	118·66		1379	250·90	107·28	143·62
1143	205·12	86·04	119·08		1383	251·68	107·64	144·04
1147	205·90	86·40	119·50		1387	252·46	108·00	144·46
1151	206·67	86·76	119·91		1391	253·23	108·36	144·87
1155	207·45	87·12	120·33		1395	254·01	108·72	145·29
1159	208·22	87·48	120·74		1399	254·78	109·08	145·70
1163	209·00	87·84	121·16		1403	255·56	109·44	146·12
1167	209·78	88·20	121·58		1407	256·34	109·80	146·54
1171	210·55	88·56	121·99		1411	257·11	110·16	146·95
1175	211·33	88·92	122·41		1415	257·89	110·52	147·37
1179	212·10	89·28	122·82		1419	258·66	110·88	147·78
1183	212·88	89·64	123·24		1423	259·44	111·24	148·20
1187	213·66	90·00	123·66		1427	260·22	111·60	148·62
1191	214·43	90·36	124·07		1431	260·99	111·96	149·03
1195	215·21	90·72	124·49		1435	261·77	112·32	149·45
1199	215·98	91·08	124·90		1439	262·54	112·68	149·86
1203	216·76	91·44	125·32		1443	263·32	113·04	150·28
1207	217·54	91·80	125·74		1447	264·10	113·40	150·70
1211	218·31	92·16	126·15		1451	264·87	113·76	151·11
1215	219·09	92·52	126·57		1455	265·65	114·12	151·53
1219	219·86	92·88	126·98		1459	266·42	114·48	151·94
1223	220·64	93·24	127·40		1463	267·20	114·84	152·36
1227	221·42	93·60	127·82		1467	267·98	115·20	152·78
1231	222·19	93·96	128·23		1471	268·75	115·56	153·19
1235	222·97	94·32	128·65		1475	269·53	115·92	153·61
1239	223·74	94·68	129·06		1479	270·30	116·28	154·02
1243	224·52	95·04	129·48		1483	271·08	116·64	154·44
1247	225·30	95·40	129·90		1487	271·86	117·00	154·86
1251	226·07	95·76	130·31		1491	272·63	117·36	155·27
1255	226·85	96·12	130·73		1495	273·41	117·72	155·69
1259	227·62	96·48	131·14		1499	274·18	118·08	156·10
1263	228·40	96·84	131·56		1503	274·96	118·44	156·52
1267	229·18	97·20	131·98		1507	275·74	118·80	156·94
1271	229·95	97·56	132·39		1511	276·51	119·16	157·35

* for information only — Do not enter on P11

Deductions Working Sheet P11	Year to 5 April 19 ___		[EXTRACT]

Employer's name **Family Favourites**

Tax District and reference **FF 464/327**

Complete only for occupational pension schemes newly contracted-out since January 1986.
Scheme contracted-out number

S	4						

Employee's surname *in CAPITALS*	SIMS	First two forenames	ROGER BRIAN

National Insurance no.	Date of birth *in figures* Day Month Year	Works no. etc	Date of leaving *in figures* Day Month Year
ZM 10 62 71 A	29 12 48	01	

Tax code †	Amended code †			
525 H	Wk/Mth in which applied			

Month no	Week no	Pay in the week or month including Statutory Sick Pay/Statutory Maternity pay 2	Total pay to date 3	Total free pay to date (Table A) 4a	K codes only Total 'additional pay' to date (Table A) 4b	Total taxable pay to date i.e. column 3 *minus* column 4a or column 3 *plus* column 4b 5	Total tax due to date as shown by Taxable Pay Tables 6	K codes only Tax due at end of current period. Mark refunds 'R' 6a	Regulatory limit i.e. 50% of column 2 entry 6b	Tax deducted or refunded in the week or month. Mark refunds 'R' 7
Bt fwd	Bt fwd	£	£	£	£	£	£	£	£	£
11	47	712 00	8637 60	4829 11		3808 49	837 41			
12	52									

Pay and Tax totals
Previous employments

This employment
Mark net refund 'R'

Where you are using a K code enter total of the amounts in column 7 for employment

National Insurance contributions

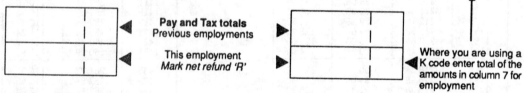

For employer's use	Earnings on which employee's contributions payable 1a	Earnings on which employee's and employer's contributions payable 1b	Employee's contributions payable 1c	Earnings on which employee's contributions at contracted-out rate payable included in column 1c 1d	Employee's contributions at contracted-out rate included in column 1c 1e	Statutory Sick Pay in the week or month included in column 2 1f	Statutory Sick Pay recovered. Only complete this if you are claiming Small Employer's Relief. 1g	Statutory Maternity Pay in the week or month included in column 2 1h	Month no	Week no
	Bt fwd £	Bt fwd £	Bt fwd £	Bt fwd £	Bt fwd £	Bt fwd £	Bt fwd £	Bt fwd £	Bt fwd	Bt fwd
fwd	8637	1332 65	590 04						11	47
									12	52
							SSP total	SMP total		

Deductions Working Sheet P11   Year to 5 April 19 ___

[EXTRACT]

Employer's name   **Family Favourites**

Tax District and reference   **FF 464/327**

Complete only for occupational pension schemes newly contracted-out since January 1986.
Scheme contracted-out number

S	4						

Employee's surname *in CAPITALS*   **SUNTER**   First two forenames   **BARBARA MARY**

National Insurance no.   **TL 71 82 03 A**

Date of birth *in figures* Day **12** Month **01** Year **37**

Works no. etc   **02**

Date of leaving *in figures* Day Month Year

Tax code †   **344L**   Amended code †

Wk/Mth in which applied

Month no	Week no	Pay in the week or month including Statutory Sick Pay/Statutory Maternity pay 2 £	Total pay to date 3 £	Total free pay to date (Table A) 4a £	Total 'additional pay' to date (Table A) 4b £	Total taxable pay to date i.e. column 3 minus column 4a or column 3 plus column 4b 5 £	Total tax due to date as shown by Taxable Pay Tables 6 £	Tax due at end of current period. Mark refunds 'R' 6a £	Regulatory limit i.e. 50% of column 2 entry 6b £	Tax deducted or refunded in the week or month. Mark refunds 'R' 7 £
Bt fwd	Bt fwd									
11	47	263 16	2894 76	3161 62		NIL	NIL			NIL
12	52									

Pay and Tax totals
Previous employments
◀ ▶
This employment
Mark net refund 'R'

Where you are using a K code enter total of the amounts in column 7 for employment

National Insurance contributions

For employer's use	Earnings on which employee's contributions payable 1a	Earnings on which employee's and employer's contributions payable 1b	Employee's contributions payable 1c	Earnings on which employee's contributions at contracted-out rate payable included in column 1c 1d	Employee's contributions at contracted-out rate included in column 1c 1e	Statutory Sick Pay in the week or month included in column 2 1f	Statutory Sick Pay recovered. Only complete this if you are claiming Small Employer's Relief. 1g	Statutory Maternity Pay in the week or month included in column 2 1h	Month no	Week no
	Bt fwd £	Bt fwd £	Bt fwd £	Bt fwd £	Bt fwd £	Bt fwd £	Bt fwd £	Bt fwd £	Bt fwd	Bt fwd
bfwd	2894	209 33	82 76						11	47
									12	52

SSP total   SMP total

115

Deductions Working Sheet P11   Year to 5 April 19 ___

Employer's name   *Family Favourites*

Tax District and reference   *FF 464 / 327*

Complete only for occupational pension schemes newly contracted-out since January 1986.
Scheme contracted-out number

S	4					

Employee's surname *in CAPITALS*   **BROOKER**   First two forenames   **MARION**

National Insurance no.	Date of birth *in figures*			Works no. etc	Date of leaving *in figures*		
	Day	Month	Year		Day	Month	Year
TZ 01 22 34 A	29	03	39	O4			

Tax code †	Amended code †				
344 L	Wk/Mth in which applied				

Month no	Week no	Pay in the week or month including Statutory Sick Pay/Statutory Maternity pay 2	Total pay to date 3	Total free pay to date (Table A) 4a	**K codes only** Total 'additional pay' to date (Table A) 4b	Total taxable pay to date i.e. column 3 *minus* column 4a or column 3 *plus* column 4b 5	Total tax due to date as shown by Taxable Pay Tables 6	**K codes only** Tax due at end of current period. Mark refunds 'R' 6a	Regulatory limit i.e. 50% of column 2 entry 6b	Tax deducted or refunded in the week or month. Mark refunds 'R' 7
Bt fwd	Bt fwd	£	£	£	£	£	£	£	£	£
11	47	693 33	1626 63	3,161 62		4465 01	991 25			
12	52									

Pay and Tax totals
Previous employments

This employment
Mark net refund 'R'

Where you are using a K code enter total of the amounts in column 7 for employment

National Insurance contributions

For employer's use	Earnings on which employee's contributions payable 1a	Earnings on which employee's and employer's contributions payable 1b	Employee's contributions payable 1c	Earnings on which employee's contributions at contracted-out rate payable included in column 1c 1d	Employee's contributions at contracted-out rate included in column 1c 1e	Statutory Sick Pay in the week or month included in column 2 1f	Statutory Sick Pay recovered. Only complete this if you are claiming Small Employer's Relief. 1g	Statutory Maternity Pay in the week or month included in column 2 1h	Month no	Week no
	Bt £ fwd	Bt £ fwd	Bt £ fwd	Bt £ fwd	Bt £ fwd	Bt £ fwd	Bt £ fwd	Bt £ fwd	Bt fwd	Bt fwd
bfwd	1626	1154 56	476 96						11	47
									12	52

SSP total

SMP total

Deductions Working Sheet P11   Year to 5 April 19 ___

Employer's name   *family favourites*

Tax District and reference   *FF 464/327*

Complete only for occupational pension schemes newly contracted-out since January 1986. Scheme contracted-out number								
S	4							

Employee's surname *in CAPITALS*   **O'MARA**   First two forenames   **MAUREEN**

National Insurance no.	Date of birth *in figures* Day Month Year	Works no. etc	Date of leaving *in figures* Day Month Year
LM 21 31 72 A	13 08 75	05	

Tax code †	Amended code †				
344 L	Wk/Mth in which applied				

Month no	Week no	Pay in the week or month including Statutory Sick Pay/Statutory Maternity pay 2	Total pay to date 3	Total free pay to date (Table A) 4a	K codes only Total 'additional pay' to date (Table A) 4b	Total taxable pay to date i.e. column 3 *minus* column 4a or column 3 *plus* column 4b 5	Total tax due to date as shown by Taxable Pay Tables 6	K codes only Tax due at end of current period. Mark refunds 'R' 6a	Regulatory limit i.e. 50% of column 2 entry 6b	Tax deducted or refunded in the week or month. Mark refunds 'R' 7
Bt fwd	Bt fwd	£	£	£	£	£	£	£	£	£
11	47	480 00	5640 00	3161 62		2478 38	495 67			
12	52									

	◄ **Pay and Tax totals** Previous employments ►		
	◄ This employment *Mark net refund 'R'* ►		◄ Where you are using a K code enter total of the amounts in column 7 for employment

National Insurance contributions

For employer's use	Earnings on which employee's contributions payable 1a	Earnings on which employee's and employer's contributions payable 1b	Employee's contributions payable 1c	Earnings on which employee's contributions at contracted-out rate payable included in column 1c 1d	Employee's contributions at contracted-out rate included in column 1c 1e	Statutory Sick Pay in the week or month included in column 2 1f	Statutory Sick Pay recovered. Only complete this if you are claiming Small Empolyer's Relief. 1g	Statutory Maternity Pay in the week or month included in column 2 1h	Month no	Week no
	Bt £ fwd	Bt £ fwd	Bt £ fwd	Bt £ fwd	Bt £ fwd	Bt £ fwd	Bt £ fwd	Bt £ fwd	Bt fwd	Bt fwd
bfwd	5640	693 22	320 76						11	47
									12	52
					▲ SSP total		▲ SMP total		

Deductions Working Sheet P11   Year to 5 April 19 ___

Employer's name   *Family Favourites*

Tax District and reference   FF 464/327

Complete only for occupational pension schemes newly contracted-out since January 1986.
Scheme contracted-out number

S	4					

Employee's surname *in CAPITALS*   SUMMERS   First two forenames   JONATHON

National Insurance no.	Date of birth *in figures*			Works no. etc	Date of leaving *in figures*		
	Day	Month	Year		Day	Month	Year
TL 33 21 72 A	27	03	70	06			

Tax code †	Amended code †				
344L	Wk/Mth in which applied				

Month no	Week no	Pay in the week or month including Statutory Sick Pay/Statutory Maternity pay 2	Total pay to date 3	Total free pay to date (Table A) 4a	**K codes only** Total 'additional pay' to date (Table A) 4b	Total taxable pay to date i.e. column 3 *minus* column 4a or column 3 *plus* column 4b 5	Total tax due to date as shown by Taxable Pay Tables 6	**K codes only** Tax due at end of current period. Mark refunds 'R' 6a	Regulatory limit i.e. 50% of column 2 entry 6b	Tax deducted or refunded in the week or month. Mark refunds 'R' 7
Bt fwd	Bt fwd	£	£	£	£	£	£	£	£	£
11	47	318 00	3995 00	3161 12		833 38	166 68			
12	52									

◀ **Pay and Tax totals** Previous employments ▶

◀ This employment *Mark net refund 'R'* ▶

◀ Where you are using a K code enter total of the amounts in column 7 for employment

National Insurance contributions

For employer's use	Earnings on which employee's contributions payable 1a	Earnings on which employee's and employer's contributions payable 1b	Employee's contributions payable 1c	Earnings on which employee's contributions at contracted-out rate payable included in column 1c 1d	Employee's contributions at contracted-out rate included in column 1c 1e	Statutory Sick Pay in the week or month included in column 2 1f	Statutory Sick Pay recovered. Only complete this if you are claiming Small Employer's Relief. 1g	Statutory Maternity Pay in the week or month included in column 2 1h	Month no	Week no
	Bt £ fwd	Bt £ fwd	Bt £ fwd	Bt £ fwd	Bt £ fwd	Bt £ fwd	Bt £ fwd	Bt £ fwd	Bt fwd	Bt fwd
b/fwd	3995	358 93	174 24						11	47
									12	52

▲ SSP total   ▲ SMP total

Deductions Working Sheet P11   Year to 5 April 19 ___   *[EXTRACT]*

Employer's name	*Family favourites*
Tax District and reference	*FF 464/327*

Complete only for occupational pension schemes newly contracted-out since January 1986.
Scheme contracted-out number

S	4						

Employee's surname *in CAPITALS*	*SINGH*	First two forenames	*GHANJA*

National Insurance no.	Date of birth *in figures* Day Month Year	Works no. etc	Date of leaving *in figures* Day Month Year
TZ 44 71 22 A	*21 02 10*	*07*	

Tax code †	*344L*	Amended code †				
		Wk/Mth in which applied				

Month no	Week no	Pay in the week or month including Statutory Sick Pay/Statutory Maternity pay £ 2	Total pay to date £ 3	Total free pay to date (Table A) £ 4a	K codes only Total 'additional pay' to date (Table A) £ 4b	Total taxable pay to date i.e. column 3 *minus* column 4a or column 3 *plus* column 4b £ 5	Total tax due to date as shown by Taxable Pay Tables £ 6	K codes only Tax due at end of current period. Mark refunds 'R' £ 6a	Regulatory limit i.e. 50% of column 2 entry £ 6b	Tax deducted or refunded in the week or month. Mark refunds 'R' £ 7
Bt fwd	Bt fwd									
11	47	413 00	5170 00	361 62		2008 38	401 68			
12	52									

Pay and Tax totals
Previous employments
◀ ▶

This employment
Mark net refund 'R'
◀ ▶

◀ Where you are using a K code enter total of the amounts in column 7 for employment

National Insurance contributions

For employer's use	Earnings on which employee's contributions payable 1a	Earnings on which employee's and employer's contributions payable 1b	Employee's contributions payable 1c	Earnings on which employee's contributions at contracted-out rate payable included in column 1c 1d	Employee's contributions at contracted-out rate included in column 1c 1e	Statutory Sick Pay in the week or month included in column 2 1f	Statutory Sick Pay recovered. Only complete this if you are claiming Small Empolyer's Relief. 1g	Statutory Maternity Pay in the week or month included in column 2 1h	Month no	Week no
	Bt £ fwd	Bt £ fwd	Bt £ fwd	Bt £ fwd	Bt £ fwd	Bt £ fwd	Bt £ fwd	Bt £ fwd	Bt fwd	Bt fwd
									11	47
bfwd	*5170*	*617 65*	*277 20*						12	52

▲ SSP total   ▲ SMP total

Deductions Working Sheet P11   Year to 5 April 19 ___

Employer's name	*Family favourites*
Tax District and reference	*FF 464/327*

Complete only for occupational pension schemes newly contracted-out since January 1986.
Scheme contracted-out number

S	4						

Employee's surname *in CAPITALS*	*SYKES*	First two forenames	*BENJAMIN*

National Insurance no.	Date of birth *in figures* Day Month Year	Works no. etc	Date of leaving *in figures* Day Month Year
LM 22 66 13 X	*13 10 68*	*08*	

Tax code †	*344L*	Amended code †				
		Wk/Mth in which applied				

Month no	Week no	Pay in the week or month including Statutory Sick Pay/Statutory Maternity pay 2	Total pay to date 3	Total free pay to date (Table A) 4a	K codes only Total 'additional pay' to date (Table A) 4b	Total taxable pay to date i.e. column 3 *minus* column 4a or column 3 *plus* column 4b 5	Total tax due to date as shown by Taxable Pay Tables 6	K codes only Tax due at end of current period. Mark refunds 'R' 6a	Regulatory limit i.e. 50% of column 2 entry 6b	Tax deducted or refunded in the week or month. Mark refunds 'R' 7
Bt fwd	Bt fwd	£	£	£	£	£	£	£	£	£
11	47	*458 00*	*4512 00*	*3161 62*		*1350 38*	*270 07*			
12	52									

Pay and Tax totals
Previous employments

This employment
Mark net refund 'R'

Where you are using a K code enter total of the amounts in column 7 for employment

National Insurance contributions

For employer's use	Earnings on which employee's contributions payable 1a	Earnings on which employee's and employer's contributions payable 1b	Employee's contributions payable 1c	Earnings on which employee's contributions at contracted-out rate payable included in column 1c 1d	Employee's contributions at contracted-out rate included in column 1c 1e	Statutory Sick Pay in the week or month included in column 2 1f	Statutory Sick Pay recovered. Only complete this if you are claiming Small Employer's Relief. 1g	Statutory Maternity Pay in the week or month included in column 2 1h	Month no	Week no
	Bt £ fwd	Bt £ fwd	Bt £ fwd	Bt £ fwd	Bt £ fwd	Bt £ fwd	Bt £ fwd	Bt £ fwd	Bt fwd	Bt fwd
bfwd	*4512*	*424 71*	*217 80*						11	47
									12	52

SSP total

SMP total

[EXTRACT]

Deductions Working Sheet P11	Year to 5 April 19 __

Employer's name *Family Favourites*

Tax District and reference *FF 464/327*

Complete only for occupational pension schemes newly contracted-out since January 1986. Scheme contracted-out number								
S	4							

Employee's surname *in CAPITALS* **BROWNE**   **First two forenames** **PAULA ANN**

National Insurance no.	Date of birth *in figures*			Works no. etc	Date of leaving *in figures*		
	Day	Month	Year		Day	Month	Year
LD 01 11 23 A	12	10	75	09			

Tax code †	Amended code †			
344L	Wk/Mth in which applied			

Month no	Week no	Pay in the week or month including Statutory Sick Pay/Statutory Maternity pay 2	Total pay to date 3	Total free pay to date (Table A) 4a	K codes only — Total 'additional pay' to date (Table A) 4b	Total taxable pay to date i.e. column 3 *minus* column 4a or column 3 *plus* column 4b 5	Total tax due to date as shown by Taxable Pay Tables 6	K codes only — Tax due at end of current period. Mark refunds 'R' 6a	Regulatory limit i.e. 50% of column 2 entry 6b	Tax deducted or refunded in the week or month. Mark refunds 'R' 7
Bt fwd	Bt fwd	£	£	£	£	£	£	£	£	£
11	47	178 75	1974 60	3161 62		NIL	NIL			
12	52									

	◄ **Pay and Tax totals** Previous employments ►	
	◄ This employment *Mark net refund 'R'* ►	

◄ Where you are using a K code enter total of the amounts in column 7 for employment

National Insurance contributions

For employer's use	Earnings on which employee's contributions payable 1a	Earnings on which employee's and employer's contributions payable 1b	Employee's contributions payable 1c	Earnings on which employee's contributions at contracted-out rate payable included in column 1c 1d	Employee's contributions at contracted-out rate included in column 1c 1e	Statutory Sick Pay in the week or month included in column 2 1f	Statutory Sick Pay recovered. Only complete this if you are claiming Small Employer's Relief. 1g	Statutory Maternity Pay in the week or month included in column 2 1h	Month no	Week no
	Bt fwd £	Bt fwd £	Bt fwd £	Bt fwd £	Bt fwd £	Bt fwd £	Bt fwd £	Bt fwd £	Bt fwd	Bt fwd
bfwd	1974	NIL	NIL						11	47
									12	52
				▲ SSP total			▲ SMP total			

[EXTRACT]

Deductions Working Sheet P11 Year to 5 April 19 ___

Employer's name *family favourites*

Tax District and reference *FF 464/327*

Complete only for occupational pension schemes
newly contracted-out since January 1986.
Scheme contracted-out number

S	4								

Employee's surname *in CAPITALS*   First two forenames

National Insurance no.	Date of birth *in figures*			Works no. etc	Date of leaving *in figures*		
	Day	Month	Year		Day	Month	Year

Tax code †	Amended code †			
	Wk/Mth in which applied			

Month no	Week no	Pay in the week or month including Statutory Sick Pay/Statutory Maternity pay 2	Total pay to date 3	Total free pay to date (Table A) 4a	K codes only — Total 'additional pay' to date (Table A) 4b	Total taxable pay to date i.e. column 3 *minus* column 4a or column 3 *plus* column 4b 5	Total tax due to date as shown by Taxable Pay Tables 6	K codes only — Tax due at end of current period. Mark refunds 'R' 6a	Regulatory limit i.e. 50% of column 2 entry 6b	Tax deducted or refunded in the week or month. Mark refunds 'R' 7
Bt fwd	Bt fwd	£	£	£	£	£	£	£	£	£
11	47									
12	52									

◄ **Pay and Tax totals**
Previous employments ►

◄ This employment
Mark net refund 'R' ►

◄ Where you are using a K code enter total of the amounts in column 7 for employment

National Insurance contributions

For employer's use	Earnings on which employee's contributions payable 1a	Earnings on which employee's and employer's contributions payable 1b	Employee's contributions payable 1c	Earnings on which employee's contributions at contracted-out rate payable included in column 1c 1d	Employee's contributions at contracted-out rate included in column 1c 1e	Statutory Sick Pay in the week or month included in column 2 1f	Statutory Sick Pay recovered. Only complete this if you are claiming Small Empoiler's Relief. 1g	Statutory Maternity Pay in the week or month included in column 2 1h	Month no	Week no
									Bt fwd	Bt fwd
	Bt fwd £	Bt fwd £	Bt fwd £	Bt fwd £	Bt fwd £	Bt fwd £	Bt fwd £	Bt fwd £	11	47
									12	52
					▲ SSP total		▲ SMP total		

| **Deductions Working Sheet P11** Year to 5 April 19 ___ | | *[EXTRACT]* |

Employer's name *Family Favourites*

Tax District and reference *FF 464/327*

Complete only for occupational pension schemes newly contracted-out since January 1986. Scheme contracted-out number							
S	**4**						

Employee's surname *in CAPITALS* **SIMMS**   **First two forenames** **ALAN ALBERT**

National Insurance no.	Date of birth *in figures* Day Month Year	Works no. etc	Date of leaving *in figures* Day Month Year
ZX 21 07 A	29 03 52	03	

Tax code † **79L**	Amended code †				
	Wk/Mth in which applied				

Month no	Week no	Pay in the week or month including Statutory Sick Pay/Statutory Maternity pay 2 £	Total pay to date 3 £	Total free pay to date (Table A) 4a £	K codes only Total 'additional pay' to date (Table A) 4b £	Total taxable pay to date i.e. column 3 *minus* column 4a or column 3 *plus* column 4b 5 £	Total tax due to date as shown by Taxable Pay Tables 6 £	K codes only Tax due at end of current period. Mark refunds 'R' 6a £	Regulatory limit i.e. 50% of column 2 entry 6b £	Tax deducted or refunded in the week or month. Mark refunds 'R' 7 £
Bt fwd	Bt fwd									
11	47	648 06	7128 72	732 49		6396 23	1474 06			
12	52									

	Pay and Tax totals Previous employments	

This employment *Mark net refund 'R'*

Where you are using a K code enter total of the amounts in column 7 for employment

National Insurance contributions

For employer's use	Earnings on which employee's contributions payable 1a	Earnings on which employee's and employer's contributions payable 1b	Employee's contributions payable 1c	Earnings on which employee's contributions at contracted-out rate payable included in column 1c 1d	Employee's contributions at contracted-out rate included in column 1c 1e	Statutory Sick Pay in the week or month included in column 2 1f	Statutory Sick Pay recovered. Only complete this if you are claiming Small Employer's Relief. 1g	Statutory Maternity Pay in the week or month included in column 2 1h	Month no	Week no
	Bt £ fwd	Bt £ fwd	Bt £ fwd	Bt £ fwd	Bt £ fwd	Bt £ fwd	Bt £ fwd	Bt £ fwd	Bt fwd	Bt fwd
									11	47
bfwd	7128	1069 31	455 40						12	52
						SSP total		SMP total		

[EXTRACT]

Deductions Working Sheet P11	Year to 5 April 19 __

Employer's name	*Family Favourites*
Tax District and reference	*FF 464/327*

Complete only for occupational pension schemes newly contracted-out since January 1986.
Scheme contracted-out number

S	4						

Employee's surname *in CAPITALS*		First two forenames

National Insurance no.	Date of birth *in figures*			Works no. etc	Date of leaving *in figures*		
	Day	Month	Year		Day	Month	Year

Tax code †	Amended code †				
	Wk/Mth in which applied				

Month no	Week no	Pay in the week or month including Statutory Sick Pay/Statutory Maternity pay 2	Total pay to date 3	Total free pay to date (Table A) 4a	**K codes only** Total 'additional pay' to date (Table A) 4b	Total taxable pay to date i.e. column 3 *minus* column 4a or column 3 *plus* column 4b 5	Total tax due to date as shown by Taxable Pay Tables 6	**K codes only** Tax due at end of current period. Mark refunds 'R' 6a	Regulatory limit i.e. 50% of column 2 entry 6b	Tax deducted or refunded in the week or month. Mark refunds 'R' 7
Bt fwd	Bt fwd	£	£	£	£	£	£	£	£	£
11	47									
12	52									

◄ **Pay and Tax totals** Previous employments ►

This employment *Mark net refund 'R'* ►

◄ Where you are using a K code enter total of the amounts in column 7 for employment

National Insurance contributions

For employer's use	Earnings on which employee's contributions payable 1a	Earnings on which employee's and employer's contributions payable 1b	Employee's contributions payable 1c	Earnings on which employee's contributions at contracted-out rate payable included in column 1c 1d	Employee's contributions at contracted-out rate included in column 1c 1e	Statutory Sick Pay in the week or month included in column 2 1f	Statutory Sick Pay recovered. Only complete this if you are claiming Small Employer's Relief. 1g	Statutory Maternity Pay in the week or month included in column 2 1h	Month no	Week no
	Bt fwd £	Bt fwd £	Bt fwd £	Bt fwd £	Bt fwd £	Bt fwd £	Bt fwd £	Bt fwd £	Bt fwd	Bt fwd
									11	47
									12	52
						▲ SSP total		▲ SMP total		

124

| **Deductions Working Sheet P11**   Year to 5 April 19 ___ | *[EXTRACT]* |

Employer's name   *family favourites*

Tax District and reference   *FF 464/327*

| Complete only for occupational pension schemes newly contracted-out since January 1986. Scheme contracted-out number |
| S | 4 | | | | | |

| Employee's surname *in CAPITALS* | First two forenames |

| National Insurance no. | Date of birth *in figures* Day Month Year | Works no. etc | Date of leaving *in figures* Day Month Year |

| Tax code † | Amended code † | | | |
| | Wk/Mth in which applied | | | |

Month no	Week no	Pay in the week or month including Statutory Sick Pay/Statutory Maternity pay 2	Total pay to date 3	Total free pay to date (Table A) 4a	**K codes only** Total 'additional pay' to date (Table A) 4b	Total taxable pay to date i.e. column 3 *minus* column 4a or column 3 *plus* column 4b 5	Total tax due to date as shown by Taxable Pay Tables 6	**K codes only** Tax due at end of current period. Mark refunds 'R' 6a	Regulatory limit i.e. 50% of column 2 entry 6b	Tax deducted or refunded in the week or month. Mark refunds 'R' 7
Bt fwd	Bt fwd	£	£	£	£	£	£	£	£	£
11	47									
12	52									

◄ **Pay and Tax totals** Previous employments ►

◄ This employment *Mark net refund 'R'* ►

◄ Where you are using a K code enter total of the amounts in column 7 for employment

National Insurance contributions

For employer's use	Earnings on which employee's contributions payable 1a	Earnings on which employee's and employer's contributions payable 1b	Employee's contributions payable 1c	Earnings on which employee's contributions at contracted-out rate payable included in column 1c 1d	Employee's contributions at contracted-out rate included in column 1c 1e	Statutory Sick Pay in the week or month included in column 2 1f	Statutory Sick Pay recovered. Only complete this if you are claiming Small Empoyer's Relief. 1g	Statutory Maternity Pay in the week or month included in column 2 1h	Month no	Week no
	Bt fwd £	Bt fwd £	Bt fwd £	Bt fwd £	Bt fwd £	Bt fwd £	Bt fwd £	Bt fwd £	Bt fwd	Bt fwd
									11	47
									12	52

▲ SSP total   ▲ SMP total

Unit IV: Calculation of wages, Statutory Sick Pay and Statutory Maternity Pay

In this unit you will:

☐ Prepare the monthly payroll.

☐ Calculate the gross wages and salaries.

☐ Work out the required deductions for tax and NI.

☐ Calculate the net wages.

☐ Work out any S.M.P. or S.S.P requirements.

☐ Prepare a wage slip for each employee to clearly show the gross wage and the deductions.

☐ Find out the necessary payment to the Inland Revenue.

☐ Process the same information on the computer using Units 25, 26, 27 and 28 and print out the payroll and the wage slips.

☐ Print out the GIROS for each employee and the payment for the Collector of Taxes.

Activities

Task 1

Prepare an analysis sheet in the format of a wages book to show the following details: name, tax code, gross pay this month, bonus, pension, total gross pay to date, free pay, taxable pay, tax 25%, less tax paid, tax this month, employee's national insurance, total deductions, net pay, employer's national insurance.

Using the information contained in Unit 28 of Part 1, enter the employee's names and work out the gross wage for each individual.

Calculate any overtime and add it to the gross wage.

Total the gross wages plus overtime for the month.

As this is the first month of the tax year no brought forward figures apply so add up the totals for the month and ensure they cross cast.

Task 2

Turn to Table A, Pay Adjustment Tables for Month 1, at the rear of this unit and enter the total free pay to date using the employee's tax code for each case.

Deduct the Free Pay from the Total Pay to Date to calculate the Taxable Pay and check your figures by checking the totals.

The Tax for this period is calculated by comparing the taxable pay to the Table B, Subtraction Tables

Add the columns across and down to make sure your figures are correct.

Task 3

Enter the National Insurance for the month by reference to the Codes following this unit.

Make sure you enter the employees figures in the wage analysis calculation and the employers figures separately.

Add the tax and national insurance to find the total deductions, and then calculate the net pay for the month.

At this stage you will need to calculate the S.S.P. and the S.M.P. The necessary information is contained in the Social Security Booklets but you may need some guidance from your tutor for this task.

Calculate the net pay for each employee's payslip and the monthly amount payable to the Revenue.

Task 4

Use the Computer to process the Self Learning Computerised Payroll Package Modules 25, 26, 27 and 28. You can then produce the necessary print-outs to compare with your manual records.

Task 5

Finally, you need to present a file containing all the activities completed in tasks 1–4.

A brief introduction to this presentation should contain an explanation and some comments or observations for the activities you have completed.

Some things to bear in mind when compiling your file:

☐ Be as neat as you can and line up your figures to make additions and calculations easier.

☐ Make sure the columns of your Wages Book add across and down.

☐ Do your manual records compare with the Computer Produced Reports? If not, briefly explain why you think this may not be so.

☐ When you have completed all the required activities, number all the pages and include a contents page.

Note: There are no solutions to this unit in the Appendix.

Month 1
Apr 6 to May 5

TABLE A - PAY ADJUSTMENT

Code	Total pay adjustment to date £	Code	Total pay adjustment to date £	Code	Total pay adjustment to date £	Code	Total pay adjustment to date £	Code	Total pay adjustment to date £	Code	Total pay adjustment to date £	Code	Total pay adjustment to date £	Code	Total pay adjustment to date £	Code	Total pay adjustment to date £
0	NIL																
1	1.59	61	51.59	121	101.59	181	151.59	241	201.59	301	251.59	351	293.25	401	334.92	451	376.59
2	2.42	62	52.42	122	102.42	182	152.42	242	202.42	302	252.42	352	294.09	402	335.75	452	377.42
3	3.25	63	53.25	123	103.25	183	153.25	243	203.25	303	253.25	353	294.92	403	336.59	453	378.25
4	4.09	64	54.09	124	104.09	184	154.09	244	204.09	304	254.09	354	295.75	404	337.42	454	379.09
5	4.92	65	54.92	125	104.92	185	154.92	245	204.92	305	254.92	355	296.59	405	338.25	455	379.92
6	5.75	66	55.75	126	105.75	186	155.75	246	205.75	306	255.75	356	297.42	406	339.09	456	380.75
7	6.59	67	56.59	127	106.59	187	156.59	247	206.59	307	256.59	357	298.25	407	339.92	457	381.59
8	7.42	68	57.42	128	107.42	188	157.42	248	207.42	308	257.42	358	299.09	408	340.75	458	382.42
9	8.25	69	58.25	129	108.25	189	158.25	249	208.25	309	258.25	359	299.92	409	341.59	459	383.25
10	9.09	70	59.09	130	109.09	190	159.09	250	209.09	310	259.09	360	300.75	410	342.42	460	384.09
11	9.92	71	59.92	131	109.92	191	159.92	251	209.92	311	259.92	361	301.59	411	343.25	461	384.92
12	10.75	72	60.75	132	110.75	192	160.75	252	210.75	312	260.75	362	302.42	412	344.09	462	385.75
13	11.59	73	61.59	133	111.59	193	161.59	253	211.59	313	261.59	363	303.25	413	344.92	463	386.59
14	12.42	74	62.42	134	112.42	194	162.42	254	212.42	314	262.42	364	304.09	414	345.75	464	387.42
15	13.25	75	63.25	135	113.25	195	163.25	255	213.25	315	263.25	365	304.92	415	346.59	465	388.25
16	14.09	76	64.09	136	114.09	196	164.09	256	214.09	316	264.09	366	305.75	416	347.42	466	389.09
17	14.92	77	64.92	137	114.92	197	164.92	257	214.92	317	264.92	367	306.59	417	348.25	467	389.92
18	15.75	78	65.75	138	115.75	198	165.75	258	215.75	318	265.75	368	307.42	418	349.09	468	390.75
19	16.59	79	66.59	139	116.59	199	166.59	259	216.59	319	266.59	369	308.25	419	349.92	469	391.59
20	17.42	80	67.42	140	117.42	200	167.42	260	217.42	320	267.42	370	309.09	420	350.75	470	392.42
21	18.25	81	68.25	141	118.25	201	168.25	261	218.25	321	268.25	371	309.92	421	351.59	471	393.25
22	19.09	82	69.09	142	119.09	202	169.09	262	219.09	322	269.09	372	310.75	422	352.42	472	394.09
23	19.92	83	69.92	143	119.92	203	169.92	263	219.92	323	269.92	373	311.59	423	353.25	473	394.92
24	20.75	84	70.75	144	120.75	204	170.75	264	220.75	324	270.75	374	312.42	424	354.09	474	395.75
25	21.59	85	71.59	145	121.59	205	171.59	265	221.59	325	271.59	375	313.25	425	354.92	475	396.59
26	22.42	86	72.42	146	122.42	206	172.42	266	222.42	326	272.42	376	314.09	426	355.75	476	397.42
27	23.25	87	73.25	147	123.25	207	173.25	267	223.25	327	273.25	377	314.92	427	356.59	477	398.25
28	24.09	88	74.09	148	124.09	208	174.09	268	224.09	328	274.09	378	315.75	428	357.42	478	399.09
29	24.92	89	74.92	149	124.92	209	174.92	269	224.92	329	274.92	379	316.59	429	358.25	479	399.92
30	25.75	90	75.75	150	125.75	210	175.75	270	225.75	330	275.75	380	317.42	430	359.09	480	400.75
31	26.59	91	76.59	151	126.59	211	176.59	271	226.59	331	276.59	381	318.25	431	359.92	481	401.59
32	27.42	92	77.42	152	127.42	212	177.42	272	227.42	332	277.42	382	319.09	432	360.75	482	402.42
33	28.25	93	78.25	153	128.25	213	178.25	273	228.25	333	278.25	383	319.92	433	361.59	483	403.25
34	29.09	94	79.09	154	129.09	214	179.09	274	229.09	334	279.09	384	320.75	434	362.42	484	404.09
35	29.92	95	79.92	155	129.92	215	179.92	275	229.92	335	279.92	385	321.59	435	363.25	485	404.92
36	30.75	96	80.75	156	130.75	216	180.75	276	230.75	336	280.75	386	322.42	436	364.09	486	405.75
37	31.59	97	81.59	157	131.59	217	181.59	277	231.59	337	281.59	387	323.25	437	364.92	487	406.59
38	32.42	98	82.42	158	132.42	218	182.42	278	232.42	338	282.42	388	324.09	438	365.75	488	407.42
39	33.25	99	83.25	159	133.25	219	183.25	279	233.25	339	283.25	389	324.92	439	366.59	489	408.25
40	34.09	100	84.09	160	134.09	220	184.09	280	234.09	340	284.09	390	325.75	440	367.42	490	409.09
41	34.92	101	84.92	161	134.92	221	184.92	281	234.92	341	284.92	391	326.59	441	368.25	491	409.92
42	35.75	102	85.75	162	135.75	222	185.75	282	235.75	342	285.75	392	327.42	442	369.09	492	410.75
43	36.59	103	86.59	163	136.59	223	186.59	283	236.59	343	286.59	393	328.25	443	369.92	493	411.59
44	37.42	104	87.42	164	137.42	224	187.42	284	237.42	344	287.42	394	329.09	444	370.75	494	412.42
45	38.25	105	88.25	165	138.25	225	188.25	285	238.25	345	288.25	395	329.92	445	371.59	495	413.25
46	39.09	106	89.09	166	139.09	226	189.09	286	239.09	346	289.09	396	330.75	446	372.42	496	414.09
47	39.92	107	89.92	167	139.92	227	189.92	287	239.92	347	289.92	397	331.59	447	373.25	497	414.92
48	40.75	108	90.75	168	140.75	228	190.75	288	240.75	348	290.75	398	332.42	448	374.09	498	415.75
49	41.59	109	91.59	169	141.59	229	191.59	289	241.59	349	291.59	399	333.25	449	374.92	499	416.59
50	42.42	110	92.42	170	142.42	230	192.42	290	242.42	350	292.42	400	334.09	450	375.75	500	417.42
51	43.25	111	93.25	171	143.25	231	193.25	291	243.25								
52	44.09	112	94.09	172	144.09	232	194.09	292	244.09								
53	44.92	113	94.92	173	144.92	233	194.92	293	244.92								
54	45.75	114	95.75	174	145.75	234	195.75	294	245.75								
55	46.59	115	96.59	175	146.59	235	196.59	295	246.59								
56	47.42	116	97.42	176	147.42	236	197.42	296	247.42								
57	48.25	117	98.25	177	148.25	237	198.25	297	248.25								
58	49.09	118	99.09	178	149.09	238	199.09	298	249.09								
59	49.92	119	99.92	179	149.92	239	199.92	299	249.92								
60	50.75	120	100.75	180	150.75	240	200.75	300	250.75								

Pay adjustment where code exceeds 500

1. Where the code is in the range **501** to **1000** inclusive proceed as follows:

   a. Subtract **500** from the code and use the balance of the code to obtain a pay adjustment figure from the table above.

   b. Add this pay adjustment figure to the figure given in the box alongside to obtain the figure of total pay adjustment to date ● | **416.67** |

2. Where the code **exceeds 1000** follow the instructions on **page 2**.

Pages 2 and 3 tell you when to use these tables

Table B
(Tax at 25%)

Remember to use the Subtraction Tables on Page 7

Tax Due on Taxable Pay from £1 to £99

Total TAXABLE PAY to date (£)	Total TAX DUE to date (£)	Total TAXABLE PAY to date (£)	Total TAX DUE to date (£)
1	0.25	61	15.25
2	0.50	62	15.50
3	0.75	63	15.75
4	1.00	64	16.00
5	1.25	65	16.25
6	1.50	66	16.50
7	1.75	67	16.75
8	2.00	68	17.00
9	2.25	69	17.25
10	2.50	70	17.50
11	2.75	71	17.75
12	3.00	72	18.00
13	3.25	73	18.25
14	3.50	74	18.50
15	3.75	75	18.75
16	4.00	76	19.00
17	4.25	77	19.25
18	4.50	78	19.50
19	4.75	79	19.75
20	5.00	80	20.00
21	5.25	81	20.25
22	5.50	82	20.50
23	5.75	83	20.75
24	6.00	84	21.00
25	6.25	85	21.25
26	6.50	86	21.50
27	6.75	87	21.75
28	7.00	88	22.00
29	7.25	89	22.25
30	7.50	90	22.50
31	7.75	91	22.75
32	8.00	92	23.00
33	8.25	93	23.25
34	8.50	94	23.50
35	8.75	95	23.75
36	9.00	96	24.00
37	9.25	97	24.25
38	9.50	98	24.50
39	9.75	99	24.75
40	10.00		
41	10.25		
42	10.50		
43	10.75		
44	11.00		
45	11.25		
46	11.50		
47	11.75		
48	12.00		
49	12.25		
50	12.50		
51	12.75		
52	13.00		
53	13.25		
54	13.50		
55	13.75		
56	14.00		
57	14.25		
58	14.50		
59	14.75		
60	15.00		

Tax Due on Taxable Pay from £100 to £23,700

TAXABLE PAY to date (£)	TAX DUE to date (£)	TAXABLE PAY to date (£)	TAX DUE to date (£)	TAXABLE PAY to date (£)	TAX DUE to date (£)	TAXABLE PAY to date (£)	TAX DUE to date (£)
100	25.00	6100	1525.00	12100	3025.00	18100	4525.00
200	50.00	6200	1550.00	12200	3050.00	18200	4550.00
300	75.00	6300	1575.00	12300	3075.00	18300	4575.00
400	100.00	6400	1600.00	12400	3100.00	18400	4600.00
500	125.00	6500	1625.00	12500	3125.00	18500	4625.00
600	150.00	6600	1650.00	12600	3150.00	18600	4650.00
700	175.00	6700	1675.00	12700	3175.00	18700	4675.00
800	200.00	6800	1700.00	12800	3200.00	18800	4700.00
900	225.00	6900	1725.00	12900	3225.00	18900	4725.00
1000	250.00	7000	1750.00	13000	3250.00	19000	4750.00
1100	275.00	7100	1775.00	13100	3275.00	19100	4775.00
1200	300.00	7200	1800.00	13200	3300.00	19200	4800.00
1300	325.00	7300	1825.00	13300	3325.00	19300	4825.00
1400	350.00	7400	1850.00	13400	3350.00	19400	4850.00
1500	375.00	7500	1875.00	13500	3375.00	19500	4875.00
1600	400.00	7600	1900.00	13600	3400.00	19600	4900.00
1700	425.00	7700	1925.00	13700	3425.00	19700	4925.00
1800	450.00	7800	1950.00	13800	3450.00	19800	4950.00
1900	475.00	7900	1975.00	13900	3475.00	19900	4975.00
2000	500.00	8000	2000.00	14000	3500.00	20000	5000.00
2100	525.00	8100	2025.00	14100	3525.00	20100	5025.00
2200	550.00	8200	2050.00	14200	3550.00	20200	5050.00
2300	575.00	8300	2075.00	14300	3575.00	20300	5075.00
2400	600.00	8400	2100.00	14400	3600.00	20400	5100.00
2500	625.00	8500	2125.00	14500	3625.00	20500	5125.00
2600	650.00	8600	2150.00	14600	3650.00	20600	5150.00
2700	675.00	8700	2175.00	14700	3675.00	20700	5175.00
2800	700.00	8800	2200.00	14800	3700.00	20800	5200.00
2900	725.00	8900	2225.00	14900	3725.00	20900	5225.00
3000	750.00	9000	2250.00	15000	3750.00	21000	5250.00
3100	775.00	9100	2275.00	15100	3775.00	21100	5275.00
3200	800.00	9200	2300.00	15200	3800.00	21200	5300.00
3300	825.00	9300	2325.00	15300	3825.00	21300	5325.00
3400	850.00	9400	2350.00	15400	3850.00	21400	5350.00
3500	875.00	9500	2375.00	15500	3875.00	21500	5375.00
3600	900.00	9600	2400.00	15600	3900.00	21600	5400.00
3700	925.00	9700	2425.00	15700	3925.00	21700	5425.00
3800	950.00	9800	2450.00	15800	3950.00	21800	5450.00
3900	975.00	9900	2475.00	15900	3975.00	21900	5475.00
4000	1000.00	10000	2500.00	16000	4000.00	22000	5500.00
4100	1025.00	10100	2525.00	16100	4025.00	22100	5525.00
4200	1050.00	10200	2550.00	16200	4050.00	22200	5550.00
4300	1075.00	10300	2575.00	16300	4075.00	22300	5575.00
4400	1100.00	10400	2600.00	16400	4100.00	22400	5600.00
4500	1125.00	10500	2625.00	16500	4125.00	22500	5625.00
4600	1150.00	10600	2650.00	16600	4150.00	22600	5650.00
4700	1175.00	10700	2675.00	16700	4175.00	22700	5675.00
4800	1200.00	10800	2700.00	16800	4200.00	22800	5700.00
4900	1225.00	10900	2725.00	16900	4225.00	22900	5725.00
5000	1250.00	11000	2750.00	17000	4250.00	23000	5750.00
5100	1275.00	11100	2775.00	17100	4275.00	23100	5775.00
5200	1300.00	11200	2800.00	17200	4300.00	23200	5800.00
5300	1325.00	11300	2825.00	17300	4325.00	23300	5825.00
5400	1350.00	11400	2850.00	17400	4350.00	23400	5850.00
5500	1375.00	11500	2875.00	17500	4375.00	23500	5875.00
5600	1400.00	11600	2900.00	17600	4400.00	23600	5900.00
5700	1425.00	11700	2925.00	17700	4425.00	23700	5925.00
5800	1450.00	11800	2950.00	17800	4450.00		
5900	1475.00	11900	2975.00	17900	4475.00		
6000	1500.00	12000	3000.00	18000	4500.00		

Where the exact amount of taxable pay is not shown, add together the figures for two (or more) entries to make up the amount of taxable pay to the nearest £1 below

6

Table B Subtraction Tables
(Lower Rate Relief)

Do not use the subtraction tables for code BR

For all ordinary suffix codes and prefix K codes - When you have used the table on Page 6 to work out the tax at 25% refer to the tables below to give the benefit of the lower rate band. Find the week or month in which the pay day falls (it is the same week or month you have used in Tables A) and **subtract** the amount shown to arrive at the tax due.

There is an example below and further examples on Page 8

Employee paid at Weekly rates

Week No.	Amount to subtract £
1	2.89
2	5.77
3	8.66
4	11.54
5	14.43
6	17.31
7	20.20
8	23.08
9	25.97
10	28.85
11	31.74
12	34.62
13	37.50
14	40.39
15	43.27
16	46.16
17	49.04
18	51.93
19	54.81
20	57.70
21	60.58
22	63.47
23	66.35
24	69.24
25	72.12
26	75.00
27	77.89
28	80.77
29	83.66
30	86.54
31	89.43
32	92.31
33	95.20
34	98.08
35	100.97
36	103.85
37	106.74
38	109.62
39	112.50
40	115.39
41	118.27
42	121.16
43	124.04
44	126.93
45	129.81
46	132.70
47	135.58
48	138.47
49	141.35
50	144.24
51	147.12
52	150.00

Employee paid at Monthly rates

Month No.	Amount to subtract
1	12.50
2	25.00
3	37.50
4	50.00
5	62.50
6	75.00
7	87.50
8	100.00
9	112.50
10	125.00
11	137.50
12	150.00

Use of Table B   *Example 1*

Employee's code is **344L**
The payment is made in **Week 7**

Pay in the week	£ 200
Previous pay to date	£1200
Total pay to date	£1400
Less free pay in Week 7 (from Table A)	£ 464.31
Total taxable pay to date	**£ 935.69**

The tax is worked out by first looking in Table B on Page 6 for the nearest round figure below £935

		Tax due
It is	£900	£225.00
Look in the shaded columns for the remainder	£ 35	£ 8.75
Totals	£935	£233.75

Then give the Lower Rate Relief by looking in the table on this page for Week 7 and subtract the amount from the tax due. It is £ 20.20

Total tax due to date   **£213.55**

7

A

6 April 1994 to 5 April 1995

Monthly table for not contracted-out standard rate contributions

Use this table for:

- employees who are over age 16 and under pension age

- employees who have an appropriate personal pension

Do not use this table for:

- married women and widows who pay reduced rate NICs

- employees who are over pension age

- employees for whom you hold form RD950

Completing form P11:

- enter 'A' in the space provided on the deductions working sheet P11 or substitute

- copy the figures in columns 1a, 1b and 1c to columns 1a, 1b and 1c of form P11

If the exact gross pay is not shown in the table, use the next smaller figure shown.

Earnings on which employee's contributions payable 1a	Total of employee's and employer's contributions payable 1b	Employee's contributions payable 1c	Employer's contributions*
£	£	£	£
247	13·83	4·94	8·89
251	14·65	5·54	9·11
255	15·19	5·94	9·25
259	15·74	6·34	9·40
263	16·28	6·74	9·54
267	16·82	7·14	9·68
271	17·37	7·54	9·83
275	17·91	7·94	9·97
279	18·46	8·34	10·12
283	19·00	8·74	10·26
287	19·54	9·14	10·40
291	20·09	9·54	10·55
295	20·63	9·94	10·69
299	21·18	10·34	10·84
303	21·72	10·74	10·98
307	22·26	11·14	11·12
311	22·81	11·54	11·27
315	23·35	11·94	11·41
319	23·90	12·34	11·56
323	24·44	12·74	11·70
327	24·98	13·14	11·84
331	25·53	13·54	11·99
335	26·07	13·94	12·13
339	26·62	14·34	12·28
343	27·16	14·74	12·42
347	27·70	15·14	12·56
351	28·25	15·54	12·71
355	28·79	15·94	12·85
359	29·34	16·34	13·00
363	29·88	16·74	13·14
367	30·42	17·14	13·28
371	30·97	17·54	13·43
375	31·51	17·94	13·57
379	32·06	18·34	13·72
383	32·60	18·74	13·86
387	33·14	19·14	14·00
391	33·69	19·54	14·15
395	34·23	19·94	14·29
399	34·78	20·34	14·44
403	35·32	20·74	14·58

Earnings on which employee's contributions payable 1a	Total of employee's and employer's contributions payable 1b	Employee's contributions payable 1c	Employer's contributions*
£	£	£	£
407	35·86	21·14	14·72
411	36·41	21·54	14·87
415	36·95	21·94	15·01
419	37·50	22·34	15·16
423	38·04	22·74	15·30
427	38·58	23·14	15·44
431	39·06	23·49	15·57
434	48·02	23·69	24·33
435	48·41	23·94	24·47
439	49·04	24·34	24·70
443	49·66	24·74	24·92
447	50·28	25·14	25·14
451	50·91	25·54	25·37
455	51·53	25·94	25·59
459	52·16	26·34	25·82
463	52·78	26·74	26·04
467	53·40	27·14	26·26
471	54·03	27·54	26·49
475	54·65	27·94	26·71
479	55·28	28·34	26·94
483	55·90	28·74	27·16
487	56·52	29·14	27·38
491	57·15	29·54	27·61
495	57·77	29·94	27·83
499	58·40	30·34	28·06
503	59·02	30·74	28·28
507	59·64	31·14	28·50
511	60·27	31·54	28·73
515	60·89	31·94	28·95
519	61·52	32·34	29·18
523	62·14	32·74	29·40
527	62·76	33·14	29·62
531	63·39	33·54	29·85
535	64·01	33·94	30·07
539	64·64	34·34	30·30
543	65·26	34·74	30·52
547	65·88	35·14	30·74
551	66·51	35·54	30·97
555	67·13	35·94	31·19
559	67·76	36·34	31·42

* for information only - do not enter on P11

6 April 1994 to 5 April 1995

Monthly table for not contracted-out standard rate contributions

A

Earnings on which employee's contributions payable 1a	Total of employee's and employer's contributions payable 1b	Employee's contributions payable 1c	Employer's contributions*	Earnings on which employee's contributions payable 1a	Total of employee's and employer's contributions payable 1b	Employee's contributions payable 1c	Employer's contributions*
£	£	£	£	£	£	£	£
563	68·38	36·74	31·64	799	121·22	60·34	60·88
567	69·00	37·14	31·86	803	121·92	60·74	61·18
571	69·63	37·54	32·09	807	122·62	61·14	61·48
575	70·25	37·94	32·31	811	123·33	61·54	61·79
579	70·88	38·34	32·54	815	124·03	61·94	62·09
583	71·50	38·74	32·76	819	124·74	62·34	62·40
587	72·12	39·14	32·98	823	125·44	62·74	62·70
591	72·75	39·54	33·21	827	126·14	63·14	63·00
595	73·37	39·94	33·43	831	126·85	63·54	63·31
599	74·00	40·34	33·66	835	127·55	63·94	63·61
603	74·62	40·74	33·88	839	128·26	64·34	63·92
607	75·24	41·14	34·10	843	128·96	64·74	64·22
611	75·87	41·54	34·33	847	129·66	65·14	64·52
615	76·49	41·94	34·55	851	130·37	65·54	64·83
619	77·12	42·34	34·78	855	131·07	65·94	65·13
623	77·74	42·74	35·00	859	131·78	66·34	65·44
627	78·21	43·04	35·17	863	132·48	66·74	65·74
629	91·12	43·24	47·88	867	155·78	67·14	88·64
631	91·65	43·54	48·11	871	156·59	67·54	89·05
635	92·35	43·94	48·41	875	157·39	67·94	89·45
639	93·06	44·34	48·72	879	158·20	68·34	89·86
643	93·76	44·74	49·02	883	159·01	68·74	90·27
647	94·46	45·14	49·32	887	159·82	69·14	90·68
651	95·17	45·54	49·63	891	160·63	69·54	91·09
655	95·87	45·94	49·93	895	161·43	69·94	91·49
659	96·58	46·34	50·24	899	162·24	70·34	91·90
663	97·28	46·74	50·54	903	163·05	70·74	92·31
667	97·98	47·14	50·84	907	163·86	71·14	92·72
671	98·69	47·54	51·15	911	164·67	71·54	93·13
675	99·39	47·94	51·45	915	165·47	71·94	93·53
679	100·10	48·34	51·76	919	166·28	72·34	93·94
683	100·80	48·74	52·06	923	167·09	72·74	94·35
687	101·50	49·14	52·36	927	167·90	73·14	94·76
691	102·21	49·54	52·67	931	168·71	73·54	95·17
695	102·91	49·94	52·97	935	169·51	73·94	95·57
699	103·62	50·34	53·28	939	170·32	74·34	95·98
703	104·32	50·74	53·58	943	171·13	74·74	96·39
707	105·02	51·14	53·88	947	171·94	75·14	96·80
711	105·73	51·54	54·19	951	172·75	75·54	97·21
715	106·43	51·94	54·49	955	173·55	75·94	97·61
719	107·14	52·34	54·80	959	174·36	76·34	98·02
723	107·84	52·74	55·10	963	175·17	76·74	98·43
727	108·54	53·14	55·40	967	175·98	77·14	98·84
731	109·25	53·54	55·71	971.	176·79	77·54	99·25
735	109·95	53·94	56·01	975	177·59	77·94	99·65
739	110·66	54·34	56·32	979	178·40	78·34	100·06
743	111·36	54·74	56·62	983	179·21	78·74	100·47
747	112·06	55·14	56·92	987	180·02	79·14	100·88
751	112·77	55·54	57·23	991	180·83	79·54	101·29
755	113·47	55·94	57·53	995	181·63	79·94	101·69
759	114·18	56·34	57·84	999	182·44	80·34	102·10
763	114·88	56·74	58·14	1003	183·25	80·74	102·51
767	115·58	57·14	58·44	1007	184·06	81·14	102·92
771	116·29	57·54	58·75	1011	184·87	81·54	103·33
775	116·99	57·94	59·05	1015	185·67	81·94	103·73
779	117·70	58·34	59·36	1019	186·48	82·34	104·14
783	118·40	58·74	59·66	1023	187·29	82·74	104·55
787	119·10	59·14	59·96	1027	188·10	83·14	104·96
791	119·81	59·54	60·27	1031	188·91	83·54	105·37
795	120·51	59·94	60·57	1035	189·71	83·94	105·77

* for information only - do not enter on P11

Page 15

Unit V: Purchase and sales ledger control accounts

A satisfactory completion of this Unit could be used for NVQ Level 2 Unit 2

The additional February data is slightly more complex and can be obtained by completing the same requirements for the February records in Part 1.

In this unit you will:

☐ Prepare a Purchase Ledger Control Account.

☐ Prepare a Sales Ledger Control Account.

☐ Total the control accounts and agree the balancing figure with the total of the sales and purchase ledgers.

☐ Process on the computer Units 3 to 8 of Part 1.

☐ Print out the Sales and Purchase Ledger Control Accounts.

Activities

Task 1

Draw up a Purchase Ledger Control Account.

Taking the information from Unit 3.3 page 12, enter the opening creditors balances as a credit.

Enter as a credit the total purchases including the VAT from the Purchase Day Book as calculated in Unit I page 100.

An opposite entry should be made for the Returns Outward Book.

Total the cheques or cash paid to suppliers from the Cash Book as a debit entry.

Find the Purchase Control Account balancing figure by adding down the highest column (it should be the credit side) and then deduct the debit balances.

The balancing figure represents the creditors, and this should agree with the ledger balances calculated in Unit 1. This balance is then carried down to the next month as a credit. Any debit balances in the purchase ledger should be entered separately as a debit total.

Task 2

Draw up a Sales Ledger Account to show debits on left hand side and credits on the right. Enter the opening debtor balance from Unit 3.3 page 12 on the Debit side of the control account.

Enter the total sales including VAT as a debit from the Sales Day Book in Unit I page 100. An opposite entry should be made for any returns outwards.

Next, from the cash book, enter the total of cheques, giros or cash received from customers as a credit.

To find the Sales Ledger Control Account balance adopt the same method as Task 1 except this time the largest column should be the debit.

The balancing figure of debtors should agree with the total of the sales ledgers as calculated in Unit I and is carried down as a debit in the next month.

Task 3

After completion of the above tasks, compare your workings with the suggested solutions for Units I and V (pages 146 and 153) to check the arithmetical accuracy of your ledgers.

Print out the Purchase and Sales Ledger Control Accounts for comparison with your workings. Note how the control account balances provide the creditors and debtors figures in the Trial Balance in Unit 8.2 page 36.

Task 4

After completion of these tasks you can repeat the same activities with the February transactions as contained in Part 1 Units 14–18. You may need some help from your tutor with this task as no solutions are given and contra entries and bad debts are introduced.

Compare your working papers with the computer printouts you produce.

Task 5

Finally, you need to present a file containing all the activities in tasks 1 to 4.

A brief introduction to this presentation should contain an explanation of why you consider control accounts are necessary.

Some things to consider when compiling your file:
❐ Try to be as neat as possible.
❐ Make sure your manual records agree with your computer produced reports. If they do not explain any differences.
❐ When you have completed all activities number all the pages and include a contents page.

Unit VI: Extended trial balance, trading & profit and loss account and balance sheet

This Unit is designed to supplement the activities required for NVQ Level 3, Unit 5, and also covers Unit 7. The additional February data is a slightly more complex and can be obtained by completing the same requirements for Unit 17 and 18 of Part 1

In this unit you will:
❐ Prepare a worksheet for an Extended Trial Balance and enter the Trial Balance figures at the period end.
❐ Correctly calculate and enter all the necessary provisions and adjustments. Add the Trial Balance and the adjustment figures across to produce an Extended Trial Balance.

❏ Analyse the Extended Trial Balance into two columns for the Profit and Loss Account and Balance Sheet and find the balancing figure of profit or loss. From these columns draft the Profit and Loss Account and Balance Sheet.

❏ Process the same information on the computer using the Units 9, 10, 11 and 12 from Part 1.

❏ Print out the revised Trial Balance and the Trading and Profit and Loss Account and Balance Sheet and compare.

❏ Process Unit 18 both manually and on the computer.

Activities

Task 1

Draw up a worksheet on wide column accounting analysis paper in the format of an Extended Trial Balance to allow a description column and 14 columns of figures.

In the first column of figures, enter the title Trial Balance and put in the account names and debit and credit figures from the Trial Balance in Unit 8.2.

Total the debit and credit columns and make sure they agree.

Title the next two columns Adjustments and enter the debits and credits required for closing stock and any corrections of errors (Unit 9.1 page 37 closing stock). Additional descriptions at the bottom of your list will be needed for the remaining items in this task.

The next two columns should be headed to record the Accruals and Prepayments. (Units 10.1 and 10.2 page 38).

Debit the accrual expense and credit sundry creditors

Debit sundry debtors and credit the Prepaid Expense.

Proceed to the next two columns and enter the Provisions for depreciation and bad debts.

Debit the depreciation expense and credit the required depreciation provision. Use the same procedure if a bad debt provision is required.

Add up each set of debits and credits and make sure they agree.

Task 2

You should now be able to calculate the Extended Trial Balance by adding across all the debits and credits to a final trial balance column. One figure, either a debit or a credit, is required for each account name.

Add down the Extended Trial Balance figures and investigate any difference to make sure the debits and credits columns agree.

The next two columns should be headed Profit and Loss Account and the final two columns Balance Sheet.

Ledger paper

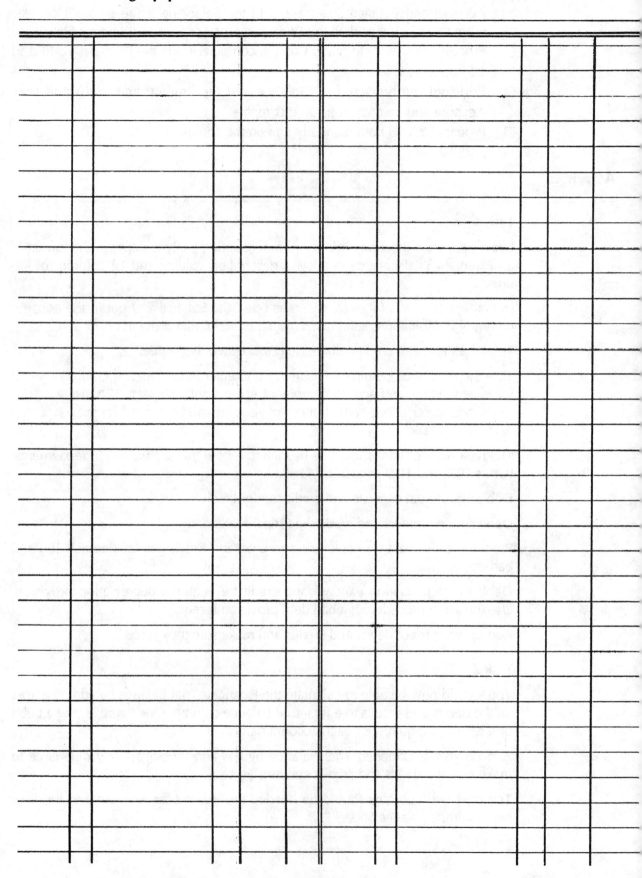

Day book

				1		2		3		4		5	
0													
1													
2													
3													
4													
5													
6													
7													
8													
9													
10													
11													
12													
13													
14													
15													
16													
17													
18													
19													
20													
21													
22													
23													
24													
25													
26													
27													
28													
29													
30													
31													
32													
33													
34													
35													
36													
37													
38													
39													

The Extended Trial Balance can now be analysed between the Profit and Loss Accounts and the Balance Sheet by entering the debits and credits in the appropriate column. Seek help from your tutor if necessary.

Add the debit and credit columns of the Profit and Loss Account columns and find out the difference. If the credits exceed the debits you have a profit, but if the debits exceed the credits you have a loss.

Enter the balancing figure to record the difference and balance the columns so that the two sides agree.

Record the double entry by including the opposite entry in the Balance Sheet columns and ensure the columns agree. Any difference must be investigated and resolved.

Task 3

Using the final balances from the Extended Trial Balance working sheet, draw up a Trading and Profit and Loss Account and Balance Sheet for the period ending 31st January 1994. Compare your results with the suggested solution in the Appendix.

Task 4

Process the same information on the computer by completing Units 9, 10, 11 and 12.

Print out an amended Trial Balance and the computerised Profit and Loss Account and Balance Sheet for comparison with your figures in tasks 1, 2 and 3.

Task 5

Complete the same activities for the next month's Extended Trial Balance and the monthly accounts using the Trial Balance produced in Unit 17.

Task 6

Finally, you need to present a file containing your completed tasks.

A brief introduction to this presentation could explain what you have done and why it is a necessary business activity.

Some things to bear in mind when compiling your file:

- ☐ Your worksheet for the Extended Trial Balance should be prepared in a reasonably neat form as though you are preparing figures for audit.
- ☐ Make sure that the Debit and Credit figures in each set of your columns agree.
- ☐ Check that your manual records agree with the computer print outs or explain any differences.
- ☐ If possible, try to prepare your introduction on a computer.

Unit VII: Stock records and stock control

A satisfactory completion of the tasks in this unit is not yet required for NVQ. Nevertheless, most accounting bodies require a good knowledge of stock control methods.

In this unit you will:
- ☐ Prepare a Stock Record Cards to show receipts and issues.
- ☐ Calculate the stock balance at the month end.
- ☐ Reconcile the stock balance to the Company's Stock Account.
- ☐ Process Units 14 to 18 on the computer from Part 1 and produce a print-out of the Stock Valuation for comparison with your stock Book.

Activities

Task 1

Prepare Stock Cards (see following page for samples) to show the date and the quantity received on the left hand side and the date and quantity issued on the right hand. A column should also be reserved for the balance in stock. A description of the item, a code or catalogue number, and the purchase price should also be included.

You can now enter the brought forward quantities on your Stock Card as at 1st February from the records contained in Part 1 (Unit 16). Make sure that the full details of each item, including the price, is recorded on the Stock Card.

Task 2

Next enter all the goods received in February from the purchase invoices in Unit 14.4 page 51. For each entry check the purchase price against the unit price to make sure it has not altered. Any alterations should be noted by updating the price on the Stock Card.

Purchase Returns must also be recorded in the issue column, (Unit 14.5 page 51).

Task 3

You should next enter the issues from stock by recording all the sales invoice details from Unit 15.

If there are any returns into stock, these should be recorded as receipts.

After each entry you can update the Stock Card balance and, if necessary, alter the sales invoice where there is insufficient stock to send.

Do not forget to reduce your Stock Records for any cash sales, (Unit 17).

Task 4

You can now attempt to value the stock by listing all the stock codes and entering the quantity and price for each category.

STOCK RECORD CARD

Stock Description ....

Stock units ....   Minimum ....

Stock Ref. No. ....   Maximum ....

Location ....   Re-order level ....

Re-order quantity ....

DATE	GOODS RECEIVED		GOODS ISSUED		BALANCE
	Reference	Quantity	Reference	Quantity	

STOCK RECORD CARD

Stock Description ....

Stock units ....   Minimum ....

Stock Ref. No. ....   Maximum ....

Location ....   Re-order level ....

Re-order quantity ....

DATE	GOODS RECEIVED		GOODS ISSUED		BALANCE
	Reference	Quantity	Reference	Quantity	

Extend the quantity and unit price to determine the stock value by category and total.

In practice these items could then be checked with the physical stock in the warehouse. Some companies would do this on a rota basis so that each item of stock is reconciled to the Stock Card on a regular basis and any discrepancies investigated.

Task 5

Compare your records with the suggested solutions in the Appendix, and then use the computer to process Units 14 to 17 of Part 1 to produce the required print outs for comparison with your stock valuation.

Task 6

Finally you need to present a file containing Tasks 1 to 6.

A brief introduction to your presentation should explain what you have done, and why you consider this is a necessary business activity.

Some things you need to bear in mind when you are compiling your file:
☐ Produce neat readable Stock Cards.
☐ Make sure sufficient detail is included to enable the tracing and auditing of documents.
☐ Check all balances and calculations.
☐ Do the computer reports agree with the reportsyou have made?
☐ When you have finished, number all the pages and draw up a Contents Page.

Unit VIII: Preparation of the quarterly VAT return

This Unit is designed to supplement the activities required for NVQ Level 3, Unit 8.

In this unit you will:
☐ Prepare a control account for the months transactions for VAT and enter the figures for the period.
☐ Correctly identify the source of VAT inputs and outputs from the January records in Part 1.
☐ Book and record all the necessary items.
☐ Calculate the net figure of VAT and compare it to the Trial Balance in Unit 8.2 page 00.
☐ Print out the VAT Control Account for the Month for comparison with your handwritten record.
☐ Complete the same activities for the month of February and prepare the quarterly VAT Return.

Activities

Task 1

Draw up a VAT Control Account to show Inputs Tax on the left hand side and Outputs Tax on the right hand side. Allow for the date and a description column on both sides.

Enter the balance from the previous month, as shown in Unit 3.3 page 12, as the first entry on the right hand side.

Calculate the VAT entry for the January purchases from the Purchase Day Book (Unit I page 100) and deduct the VAT on the Returns Inward Book. Enter the net figure as an input on the VAT Control Account.

Find out the VAT sales figure from the Sales Day Book (as shown in Unit I page 100) and this time deduct the VAT on the Returns Inwards to calculate the net output figure. You should enter this as the output figure for sales on the right of the VAT Control Account.

Task 2

Next you should find out the VAT inputs and outputs on the cash transactions. This can be found from the petty cash transaction in Part 1 Unit 6 (Unit II page 101).

Enter the Petty Cash Total for VAT inputs on the left hand side of the VAT Control Account and the total VAT for Cash Sales as an output on the right.

Finally you need to calculate the inputs on the expenses for January by listing the VAT for the items in Part 1 Unit 7. Enter the expenses VAT as inputs on the left.

You should now be able to calculate the balancing figure for the VAT Control

Account by adding down the inputs and outputs figures and carrying down the balancing figure.

This should represent the amount the business owes, or is owed, by Customs and Excise and should compare to the VAT entry in the Trial Balance in Unit 8.3.

Task 3

Print out the VAT Control Account from the Nominal Ledger and compare it with your manual records.

Task 4

You can now attempt the same activities for the month of February by processing Units 14 to 19.

From the information contained in Unit 19 you should now be able to complete and reconcile the VAT return on the following page for the three months to the end of February.

Task 5

Finally, you need to present a file containing your completed tasks.

A brief introduction to this presentation should explain what you have done and why it is a necessary business activity.

Some things to bear in mind when compiling your file:

☐ You should draw up a worksheet showing the manual VAT Control Accounts for January and February.

☐ This should be prepared neatly, as though you are preparing figures for Customs and Excise.

☐ Include all the Tasks and the completed VAT Return.

☐ Check that your manual records agree with the computer print outs or explain any differences.

☐ If possible, try to word process your introduction on a computer.

Now that you are familiar with computerised accounting using Sage, you can turn back to Part 1 and do Units 13 and 20 for which there is no manual alternative.

HM Customs and Excise

Value Added Tax Return
For the period
to

01.12.93 to 28.2.94

Registration number	Period
843-62957	02

You could be liable to a financial penalty if your completed return and all the VAT payable are not received by the due date.

Due date:

For official use D O R only	

Family Favourites
Lichfield Industrial Estate
Tamworth
Staffordshire

Fold here

Before you fill in this form please read the notes on the back and the VAT Leaflet *"Filling in your VAT return"*. Complete all boxes clearly in ink, writing 'none' where necessary. Don't put a dash or leave any box blank. If there are no pence write "00" in the pence column. Do not enter more than one amount in any box.

For official use			£	p
	VAT due in this period on **sales** and other outputs	1		
	VAT reclaimed in this period on **purchases** and other inputs	2		
	Net VAT to be paid to Customs or reclaimed by you (**Difference between boxes 1 and 2**)	3		
	Total value of **sales** and all other outputs excluding any VAT. **Include your box 6 figure**	4		00
	Total value of **purchases** and all other inputs excluding any VAT. **Include your box 7 figure**	5		00
	Total value of all **sales** and related services to other EC Member States	6		00
	Total value of all **purchases** and related services from other EC Member States	7		00

Retail schemes. If you have used any of the schemes in the period covered by this return please enter the appropriate letter(s) in this box.

If you are enclosing a payment please tick this box.

DECLARATION by the signatory to be completed by or on behalf of the person named above.

I, ...declare that the
(Full name of signatory in BLOCK LETTERS)

information given above is true and complete.

Signature ....Date ....19...........

A false declaration can result in prosecution.

VAT 100   CD 2850/N9(02/91)   F 3790 (JANUARY 1992)

Appendix: Solutions to manual January calculations

The following suggested solutions to some of the manual calculations for January are drafted to enable accounting students to compare layouts and contents of the various tasks.

The solutions to manual calculations not found in this appendix are included in the Lecturer's Supplement.

Unit I Solutions

Task 1

PURCHASE DAY BOOK

Date	Details	Enter	Ref.	Amount	VAT	Total
Jan 1	Nikes	✓	3485	1172 50	205 19	1377 69
Jan 4	Betterwares	✓	2347	981 00	171 68	1152 68
Jan 9	Racquets & Balls	✓	P1224	1815 00	317 63	2132 63
Jan 7	Mann Richards	✓	1011	1188 55	208 00	1396 55
Jan 2	Levis	✓	P1234	454 60	79 56	534 16
Jan 5	Brittania	✓	7510	747 02	130 73	877 75
	Month Total			6358 67	1112 79	7471. 46

RETURNS OUTWARDS BOOK

Jan 16	Racquets & Balls ✓ Entry	01/16	14 00	2 45	16 45
Jan 12	Betterwares	01/12	9 25	1 62	10 87
	Month Total		23 25	4 07	27 32

Tasks 2 & 3 Purchase ledger

Betterwares

12/1 Cred	10 87	24/12 b/fwd	173 21
		4/1 Inv	1152 68
31/1 Bal C/d	1315 02		
	1325 89		1325 89
		1/2 Bal b/d	1315 02

Levis

7/1 Chq	98 64	30/11 b/fwd	98 64
		2/1 Inv	534 16
31/1 Bal C/d	534 16		
	632 80		632 80
		1/2 Bal b/d	534 16

Brittania

7/1	cheq	404 00	23/11	b/fwd	404 00
			5/1	Inv	877 75
31/1	Bal c/d	877 75			
		1281 75			1281 75
			1/2	Bal b/d	877 75

Mann Richards

			12/12	b/fwd	603 72
			7/1	Inv.	1396 55
31/1	Bal c/d	2000 27			
		2000 27			2000 27
			1/2	bal b/d	2000. 27

Nikey

			10/12	b/fwd	3521 63
			1/1	Inv	1377 69
31/1	Bal c/d	4899 32			
		4899 32			4899 32
			1/2	bal b/d	4899 32

Racquets & Balls

10/1	cheq	106 32	5/12	b/fwd	106 32
14/1	Cr.Nt	16 45	9/1	Inv	2132 63
31/1	Bal c/d	2116 18			
		2238 95			2238 95
			1/2	Bal b/d	2116 18

Task 3 List of creditors

	£
Betterwares	1315 02
Brittania	877 75
Levis	534 16
Mann Richards	2000 27
Nikey	4899 32
Racquets & Balls	2116 18
Total	11742 70

Task 4

SALES DAY BOOK

Date	Details	Ref.	Amount £	VAT £	Total £
Jan 13	Mr Whitehouse	7005	764 50	133 79	898 29
Jan 19	Mrs A Nolan	7006	503 55	88 12	591 67
Jan 22	Mrs C Evans	7007	823 08	144 04	967 12
Jan 24	Mrs M Harris	7008	256 32	44 86	301 18
Jan 3	Mrs J Whitby	7001	490 39	85 82	576 21
Jan 5	Mrs T Blankley	7002	330 91	57 91	388 82
Jan 7	Mr A Holloway	7003	1190 10	208 27	1398 37
Jan 31	Miss J Goldingay	7009	1808 64	316 51	2125 15
Jan 31	Mr P Weir	7010	2087 28	365 27	2452 55
Jan 9	Mrs J. Williams	7004	305 82	53 52	359 34
			8560 59	1498 11	10058 70

RETURNS INWARDS BOOK

			£	£	£
Jan 31	Mr P Weir	123	25 19	4 41	29 60
	Mr P Whitby	01/12	12 59	2 20	14 79
			37 78	6 61	44 39

Tasks 4 & 5 Sales ledger

Blankley

6/1 B/fwd	134 70	10/1 Cheque	134 70
5/1 Inv	388 82	31/1 Bal c/d	388 82
	523 52		523 52
1/2 bal b/d	388 82		

Holloway

7/12 B/fwd	98 62	Giro	98 62
7/1 Inv	1398 37	Bal c/d	1398 37
	1496 99		1496 99
1/2 bal b/d	1398 37		

Harris

30/11 B/fwd	60.11	5/1 Cheque	60.11
12/12 "	75.10		
24/1 Inv.	301.18	31/1 Bal c/d	376.28
	436.39		436.39
1/2 bal b/d	376.28		

Goldingay.

16/12 b/fwd	27 12		
31/1 Inv.	2125 15	31/1 Bal c/d	2152 27
	2152 27		2152 27
1/2 Bal b/d	2152 27		

Whitehouse

31/12	bfwd	86.50	31/12	Cheque	86 50
13/1	Inv	898.29	31/1	Bal c/d	898.29
		984.79			984.78
1/2	Bal b/d	898.29			

Weir

15/12	bfwd	45 07	31/1	C/N	29 60
31/1	Inv	2452 55		Bal c/d	2468 02
		2491 62			2491 62
1/2	bal b/d	2468 02			

Williams

5/11	bfwd	52.00			
6/12	"	50.37			
9/1	Inv.	359.34	31/1	Bal c/d	461 71
		461.71			461 71
1/2	bal b/d	461.71			

Evans

30/11	bfwd	73 63	4/1	cheque	73 63
22/1	Inv	967 12	31/1	Bal c/d	967 12
		1040 75			1040 75
1/2	bal b/d	967 12			

Whitby

5/11	Bfwd	29 17	31/1	C/N	14 79
3/1	Inv.	576 21	31/1	Bal c/d	590 59
		605 38			605 38
1/2	bal b/d	590 59			

Nolan

31/12	Bfwd	43 00	1/1	Cheque	40 00
14/1	Inv	591 67	31/1	Bal c/d	594 67
		634 67			634 67
1/2	Bal b/d	594 67			

Task 5 List of debtors

	£
Harris	376 28
Goldingay	2152 27
Whitehouse	898 29
Weir	2468 02
Williams	461 71
Evans	967 12
Nolan	594 67
Whitby	590 59
Holloway	1398 37
Blankley	388 82
	10296 14

Unit II Solutions

Tasks 1 & 2

CASH BOOK.

	Receipts				Payments		
Date	Details	£		Date	Details		£
Jan 1	Balance b/fwd	1020 00		Jan 10	Racquets ab 332		106 32
" -	Whitehouse	86 50		Jan 7	Lewis 331		98 64
" 1	Nolan	40 00		" 7	Britannia 334		454 00
" 5	Harris	60 11		" 1	Petty Cash 330		200 00
" 6	Evans	73 63		" 25	Electric Board 336		174 60
" 10	Blankley	134 70		" 31	B'ham Herald 338		155 25
" 31	Petty Cash	786 18		" 28	Adam Ford 339		231 60
" 31	Holloway Giro	98 62		" 31	Tamworth Svcs 337		63 25
				" 25	Adam Ford 340		112 93
				" 8	Darnhill 341		700 00
				" 17	Print on Point 342		11 50
				" 27	Wages Cheque 089		1498 06
				" 19	Inland Revenue 333		75 89
				" 31	Bank Charges D/D		31 97
				" 4	Grabbet Prop D/D		479 17
" 31	Balance c/d	2043 44					
		4343 18					4343 18
				Feb 1	Balance b/dwn		2043 44

Task 3

BANK RECONCILIATION

					£	£
Jan 31st	Balance as CASH BOOK					(2043 44)
	Add Cheques drawn but not presented					
		Bham Herald	338	155.25		
		Adam Ford	339	231 60		
		Tamworth Svcs	337	63 25		
		Wages	089	1498 06	1948 16	
						(95 28)
	Less Receipts not on Bank Statement					
		Blankley		134 70		
		Petty Cash		786 18	920 88	
Jan 31st	Balance at BANK					(1016 16)

Tasks 4 & 5 Petty cash book

Code	Receipts £	Date	DETAILS	Voucher No	Total Payments £	Office Stationery £	Postage £	Cleaning £	Sundries £	Petrol £	VAT £
(13b)	200 00	Jan 1	Balance b/d	—							
		Jan 1	Cash Box	1	25 60	21 79					3 81
		Jan 2	Donation	2	20 00				20 00		
		Jan 3	Petrol B781 RFA	3	13 00					11 06	1 94
		Jan 6	Fruit onProut	4	11 75	10 00					1 75
		Jan 9	Milkman	5	3 20				3 20		
		Jan 15	Postage	6	8 50		8 50				
		Jan 17	Tea Coffee Sugar	7	3 17				3 17		
		Jan 21	Petrol B781 RFA	8	15 00					12 77	2 23
		Jan 24	Window Cleaner	9	23 00			23 00			
		Jan 25	WHSmith (Pens)	10	18 70	15 91					2 79
		Jan 30	Postages	11	5 20		5 20				
		Jan 28	Petrol B781 RFA	12	23 50					20 00	3 50
		Jan 28	Total Payments		170 62	47 70	13 70	23 00	26 47	43 83	16 02
(4001)	481 34	Jan 30	Cash Sale	82		(7504)	(7501)	(7801)	(8206)	(7300)	(2200)
(4000)	475 46	Jan 30	Cash Sale	83							
		Jan 31	Total Banked		186 18						
		Jan 31	Balance c/d		200 00						
	1156 80				1156 80						
	200 00	Feb 1	Balance b/d								

Unit III Solutions

Task 1

FAMILY FAVOURITES   WAGE BOOK

March 94

			Tax Code	Gross Wage	Add Bonus	Month Total	Add Pay to date	Total Pay to date
Code	01	Roger Sims	525H	712 00	350 00	1062 00	8637 60	9699 60
"	02	Barbara Sunter	344L	250 00	25 00	275 00	2894 76	3169 76
"	03	Alan Simms	79L	650 00	65 00	715 00	1128 72	1843 72
"	04	Marion Brooker	344L	695 00	69 50	764 50	7626 63	8391 13
"	05	Maureen O'Mara	344L	480 00	48 00	528 00	5640 00	6168 00
"	06	Jonathan Summers	344L	318 00	31 80	349 80	3995 00	4344 80
"	07	Ghanja Singh	344L	413 00	41 30	454 30	5170 00	5624 30
"	08	Benjamin Sykes	344L	448 00	44 80	492 80	4512 00	5004 80
"	09	Paula Ann Brown	344L	178 75	17 88	196 63	1974 60	2171 23
		MONTH TOTAL		4144 75	693 28	4838 03	47579 31	52417 34

Ⓐ   c/down

Tasks 2 & 3

Free Pay	Taxable Pay	TAX	less before Tax	TAX This Month	N.I. Employees	Pension	Total Deductions	Net Pay
5268 12	4431 48	982 75	837 41	145 34	78 48	53 10	276 92	735 08
3449 04	(279 28)	NIL	NIL	NIL	7 92		7 92	267 08
799 08	7044 64	1636 00	1474 06	161 94	47 52	.	209 46	505 54
3449 04	4942 09	1110 50	991 25	119 25	51 84		171 09	593 41
3449 04	2718 96	554 50	495 67	58 83	30 60		89 43	438 57
3449 04	895 76	179 00	166 68	12 32	14 40		26 72	323 08
3449 04	2175 26	435 00	401 68	33 32	23 76		57 08	397 22
3449 04	1555 76	311 00	270 07	40 93	27 36		68 29	424 51
3449 04	(1277 31)	NIL	NIL	NIL	NIL		NIL	196 63
30210 48	22206 86	5208 75	4636 82	571 93	281 88	53 10	906 91	3931 12

Ⓒ   Ⓑ   Ⓕ

For a completed example of a P11 form turn to page 166.

Task 4

N.I. Employers	Total NI
110 34	188.82
12 74	20 66
61 66	109 18
65 79	117 63
34 91	66 51
16 05	30 45
29 90	53 66
32 54	59 90
-	-
363 93	645 81
(E)	(D)

Please note:

i) Small differences in the tax calculations are due to errors in the brought forward figures.

ii) The pension figure is treated separately for this example.

iii) The updated P11 sheets are contained in the Lecturer's Supplement.

iv) The Year End Tax Return is also in the Lecturer's Supplement.

v) The bookkeeping entries to record the wage entries for these entries are:

	£	£
a) Debit Wages Account	4838.03	
b) Credit Pension Control		53.10
c) Credit Taxation Control		731.31
d) Credit NHI Control		655.47
e) Debit NI Employers Cont	364.07	
f) Credit Wages Control		3762.22

Unit V Solutions

Task 1

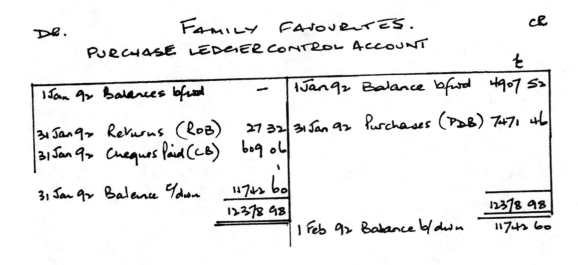

DR.   FAMILY FAVOURITES.   CR

PURCHASE LEDGER CONTROL ACCOUNT

	£		£
1 Jan 92 Balances bfwd	—	1 Jan 92 Balance bfwd	4907 52
31 Jan 92 Returns (ROB)	27 32	31 Jan 92 Purchases (PDB)	7471 46
31 Jan 92 Cheques Paid (CB)	609 06		
31 Jan 92 Balance C/dwn	11742 60		
	12378 98		12378 98
		1 Feb 92 Balance b/dwn	11742 60

Task 2

DR   FAMILY FAVOURITES   CR
SALES LEDGER CONTROL ACCOUNT

		£				£
1 Jan 92	Balances b/fwd	775 39	1 Jan 92	Balance b/fwd		—
31 Jan 92	Sales (SDB)	10058 70	31 Jan 92	Returns (RB)		44 39
			31 Jan 92	Cheques Rec'd (CB)		394 94
			31 Jan 92	Giro " (")		98 62
			31 Jan 92	Balance c/dwn		10296 14
		10834 09				10834 09
1 Feb 92	Balance b/dwn	10296 14				

Task 3

Refer to the suggested solutions for Unit I, Tasks 3 and 5.

Unit VI Solutions

Task 1 Extended Trial Balance

	Trial Balance Dr	Cr	Adjustments Dr	Cr	Accruals and Prepayments Dr	Cr
Leasehold Property	10000 00					
Motor Vehicles	5000 00					
Debtors Control Account	1029 14					
Bank Account		2043 42				
Petty Cash	200 00					
Creditors Control Account		1174 70				
VAT Tax Control		628 42				
PAYE		102 94				
National Insurance		104 00				
Capital		10000 00				
Profit & Loss Account		5303 36				
Sales: Clothes		2309 43				
Sales Sportswear		3918 16				
Sales Household		3109 52				
Opening Stock: Clothes	1587 10					
Opening Stock Sportswear	1696 50					
Opening Stock Household	728 50					
Purchases: Clothes	1201 62					
Purchases: Sportswear	2913 50					
Purchases: Household	2160 30					
Staff Wages	1653 00					
National Insurance	52 00					
Rent	479 17					
Electricity	148 60					
Fuel and Oil	240 94					
Repairs & Servicing	96 11					
Postage and Carriage	13 70					
Office Stationery	57 49					
Maintenance & Cleaning	23 00					
Bank Charges	31 97					
Advertising	185 96					
Insurance	700 00					641 67
Sundry Expenses	26 37					
Closing Stock: Clothes			1362 62			
Closing Stock: Sportswear			2309 00			
Closing Stock: Household			2345 00			
Closing Stock: Clothes				1362 62		
Closing Stock: Sportswear				2309 00		
Closing Stock: Household				2345 00		
Sundry Debtors (P.Paid)					641 67	
Sundry Creditors (Accrual)						250 00
Rates					250.00	
Depreciation Lease						
Depreciation MotorVan						
Depreciation Provision						
Profit for the Period						
	39261 97	39261 97	6016 62	6016 62	891 67	891 67

Continued on p.156

Tasks 2 & 3 Trading and Profit and Loss Account and Balance Sheet

Dr Provisions Cr		Dr Extended Trial Balance Cr		Dr Profit & Loss Cr		Dr Balance Sheet Cr	
		10000 00				10000 00	
		5000 00				5000 00	
		10296 14				10296 14	
			2043 44				2043 44
		200 00				200 00	
			11742 70				11742 70
			628 42				628 42
			102 94				102 94
			104 00				104 00
			10000 00				10000 00
			5303 36				5303 36
			2309 43			2309 43		
			3918 16			3918 16		
			3109 52			3109 52		
		1287 10		1287 10			
		1696 50		1696 50			
		738 50		738 50			
		1201 62		1201 62			
		2973 50		2973 50			
		2160 30		2160 30			
		1653 00		1653 00			
		52 00		52 00			
		479 17		479 17			
		148 60		148 60			
		240 94		240 94			
		96 11		96 11			
		13 70		13 70			
		57 49		57 49			
		23 00		23 00			
		31 97		31 97			
		185 96		185 96			
		58 33		58 33			
		26 37		26 37			
		1362 62				1362 62	
		2309 00				2309 00	
		2345 00				2345 00	
			1362 62		1362 62		
			2309 00		2309 00		
			2345 00		2345 00		
		641 67				641 67	
			250 00				250 00
		250 00		250 00			
83 33		83 33		83 33			
104 17		104 17		104 17			
	187 50	187 50					187 50
				1792 07			1792 07
187 50	187 50	45716 09	45716 09	15353 73	15353 73	32154 43	32154 43

Unit VII Solutions

Tasks 1, 2 & 3

STOCK RECORD CARD

Stock Description ..THREE PIECE SUIT..............
Stock units ....
Stock Ref. No. ...0201...
Location ....
1
Cost £9.10

DATE	GOODS RECEIVED Reference	Quantity	GOODS ISSUED Reference	Quantity	BALANCE
	Minimum				
	Maximum				
	Re-order level				
	Re-order quantity				
1.2.94	B/FWD	46			46
9.2.94	REC'D	20			66
13.2.94			SALE	20	46

STOCK RECORD CARD

Stock Description ..EMBROIDERED DRESS............
Stock units ....
Stock Ref. No. ...0202...
Location ....
1
Cost £5.90

DATE	GOODS RECEIVED Reference	Quantity	GOODS ISSUED Reference	Quantity	BALANCE
	Minimum				
	Maximum				
	Re-order level				
	Re-order quantity				
1.2.94	B/FWD	30			30
7.2.94	REC'D	15			45
13.2.94			SALE	25	20
15.2.94			SALE	15	5

STOCK RECORD CARD

Stock Description ..BEACH DRESS...........
Stock units ....
Stock Ref. No. ...0203...
Location ....
1
Cost £4.54

DATE	GOODS RECEIVED Reference	Quantity	GOODS ISSUED Reference	Quantity	BALANCE
	Minimum				
	Maximum				
	Re-order level				
	Re-order quantity				
1.2.94	B/FWD	45			45
7.2.94	REC'D	70			115
13.2.94			SALE	30	85
15.2.94			SALE	25	60

STOCK RECORD CARD

Stock Description ..PLEAT FRONT TROUSERS...
Stock units ....
Stock Ref. No. ...0402...
Location ....
1
Cost £5.90

DATE	GOODS RECEIVED Reference	Quantity	GOODS ISSUED Reference	Quantity	BALANCE
	Minimum				
	Maximum				
	Re-order level				
	Re-order quantity				
1.2.94	B/FWD	10			10
7.2.94	REC'D	20			30
4.2.94			SALE	10	20
15.2.94			SALE	15	5

STOCK RECORD CARD

Stock Description ..BRUSHED COTTON SWEATSHIRT...
Stock units ....
Stock Ref. No. ...0504...
Location ....
1
Cost £4.54

DATE	GOODS RECEIVED Reference	Quantity	GOODS ISSUED Reference	Quantity	BALANCE
	Minimum				
	Maximum				
	Re-order level				
	Re-order quantity				
1.2.94	B/FWD	35			35
9.2.94	REC'D	20			55
15.2.94	RETURN		RETURN	2	53
15.2.94			SALE	35	18

STOCK RECORD CARD

Stock Description ..THREE PIECE OFFICE SUIT...
Stock units ....
Stock Ref. No. ...0505...
Location ....
1
Cost £13.63

DATE	GOODS RECEIVED Reference	Quantity	GOODS ISSUED Reference	Quantity	BALANCE
	Minimum				
	Maximum				
	Re-order level				
	Re-order quantity				
1.2.94	B/FWD	14			14
7.2.94	REC'D	20			34
4.2.94			SALE	10	24
15.2.94			SALE	10	14

STOCK RECORD CARD

Stock Description ... WHITE BIKINI

Stock units ....

Stock Ref. No. ... 070W

Location ... 1

COST £7.00

Minimum ....
Maximum ....
Re-order level ....
Re-order quantity ....

DATE	GOODS RECEIVED		GOODS ISSUED		BALANCE
	Reference	Quantity	Reference	Quantity	
1·2·94	B/FWD	22			22
15.2.94	REC'D	30			52
27.2.94			SALE	30	22

STOCK RECORD CARD

Stock Description ... SWEATSHIRTS

Stock units ....

Stock Ref. No. ... 1105

Location ... S

Cost £4.50

Minimum ....
Maximum ....
Re-order level ....
Re-order quantity ....

DATE	GOODS RECEIVED		GOODS ISSUED		BALANCE
	Reference	Quantity	Reference	Quantity	
1·2·94	B/FWD	25			25
5.2.94	REC'D	5			30
15.2.94	REC'D	30			60
27.2.94			SALE	30	30
28.2.94			SALE	25	5

STOCK RECORD CARD

Stock Description ... HANG TEN JACKET

Stock units ....

Stock Ref. No. ... 1001

Location ... S

COST £15.00

Minimum ....
Maximum ....
Re-order level ....
Re-order quantity ....

DATE	GOODS RECEIVED		GOODS ISSUED		BALANCE
	Reference	Quantity	Reference	Quantity	
1·2·94	B/FWD	10			10
15.2.94	REC'D	20			30
27.2.94			SALE	5	25
28.2.94			SALE	15	10

STOCK RECORD CARD

Stock Description ... ADIDAS SHORTS

Stock units ....

Stock Ref. No. ... 1106

Location ... S

Cost £4.50

Minimum ....
Maximum ....
Re-order level ....
Re-order quantity ....

DATE	GOODS RECEIVED		GOODS ISSUED		BALANCE
	Reference	Quantity	Reference	Quantity	
1·2·94	B/FWD	12			12
5.2.94	REC'D	24			36
28.2.94			SALE	10	26
28.2.94			SALE	24	2

STOCK RECORD CARD

Stock Description ... LONG JOHN WET SUITS

Stock units ....

Stock Ref. No. ... 1002

Location ... S

COST £15.00 £20.00

Minimum ....
Maximum ....
Re-order level ....
Re-order quantity ....

DATE	GOODS RECEIVED		GOODS ISSUED		BALANCE
	Reference	Quantity	Reference	Quantity	
1·2·94	B/FWD	10			10
15.2.94	REC'D	20			30
27.2.94			SALE	5	25
28.2.94			SALE	15	10

STOCK RECORD CARD

Stock Description ... GREY SWEATSHIRT

Stock units ....

Stock Ref. No. ... 1107

Location ... S

Cost £5.50

Minimum ....
Maximum ....
Re-order level ....
Re-order quantity ....

DATE	GOODS RECEIVED		GOODS ISSUED		BALANCE
	Reference	Quantity	Reference	Quantity	
1·2·94	B/FWD	15			15
5.2.94	REC'D	10			25
28.2.94			SALE	15	10
20.2.94			C/SALE	10	

STOCK RECORD CARD

Stock Description ..PILOT FITNESS SHOES..........

Stock units ....

Stock Ref. No. ..1401.........

Location ......5........

Cost £17.50

	Minimum	
	Maximum	
	Re-order level	
	Re-order quantity	

DATE	GOODS RECEIVED		GOODS ISSUED		BALANCE
	Reference	Quantity	Reference	Quantity	
1-2-94	B/FWD	20			20
5-2-94	REC'D	25			45
12.2.94			SALE	10	35
27.2.94			SALE	20	15

STOCK RECORD CARD

Stock Description ..JOG PANTS..........

Stock units ....

Stock Ref. No. ..1108.........

Location ......5........

Cost £7.00

	Minimum	
	Maximum	
	Re-order level	
	Re-order quantity	

DATE	GOODS RECEIVED		GOODS ISSUED		BALANCE
	Reference	Quantity	Reference	Quantity	
1-2-94	B/FWD	40			40
15-2-94	REC'D	20			60
28.2.94			SALE	20	40
28.2.94			SALE	20	20
20.2.94			C/SALE	20	

STOCK RECORD CARD

Stock Description ..CONTINENTAL FITNESS SHOE..........

Stock units ....

Stock Ref. No. ..1402.........

Location ......5........

Cost £18.50

	Minimum	
	Maximum	
	Re-order level	
	Re-order quantity	

DATE	GOODS RECEIVED		GOODS ISSUED		BALANCE
	Reference	Quantity	Reference	Quantity	
1-2-94	B/FWD	20			20
5-2-94	REC'D	20			40
12.2.94			SALE	8	32

STOCK RECORD CARD

Stock Description ..RED SWEATSHIRT..........

Stock units ....

Stock Ref. No. ..1109.........

Location ......5........

Cost £8.50

	Minimum	
	Maximum	
	Re-order level	
	Re-order quantity	

DATE	GOODS RECEIVED		GOODS ISSUED		BALANCE
	Reference	Quantity	Reference	Quantity	
1-2-94	B/FWD	20			20
15-2-94	REC'D	10			30
28.2.94			SALE	15	15
20.2.94			C/SALE	10	5

STOCK RECORD CARD

Stock Description ..JACK RUNNING SHOES..........

Stock units ....

Stock Ref. No. ..1403.........

Location ......5........

Cost £14.00

	Minimum	
	Maximum	
	Re-order level	
	Re-order quantity	

DATE	GOODS RECEIVED		GOODS ISSUED		BALANCE
	Reference	Quantity	Reference	Quantity	
1-2-94	B/FWD	20			20
5-2-94	REC'D	20			40
12.2.94			SALE	5	35

STOCK RECORD CARD

Stock Description ..BLUE POLO SHIRTS..........

Stock units ....

Stock Ref. No. ..1110.........

Location ......5........

Cost £5.00

	Minimum	
	Maximum	
	Re-order level	
	Re-order quantity	

DATE	GOODS RECEIVED		GOODS ISSUED		BALANCE
	Reference	Quantity	Reference	Quantity	
1-2-94	B/FWD	30			30
5-2-94	REC'D	10			40
20.2.94			C/SALE	25	15

STOCK RECORD CARD

Stock Description ...50 PIECE HOUSEHOLD SET...

Stock units ....

Stock Ref. No. ...5201...

Location ....10...............

Cost £25.30

DATE	GOODS RECEIVED Reference	Quantity	GOODS ISSUED Reference	Quantity	BALANCE
1-2-94	B.FWD	3			3
1-2-94	G.REC'D	2			5
20.2.94			C/SALE	3	2

Minimum ....

Maximum ....

Re-order level ....

Re-order quantity ....

STOCK RECORD CARD

Stock Description ...SYDNEY RUNNING SHOES...

Stock units ....

Stock Ref. No. ...1404...

Location ....5...............

Cost £13.00

DATE	GOODS RECEIVED Reference	Quantity	GOODS ISSUED Reference	Quantity	BALANCE
1-2-94	B/FWD	20			20
5-2-94	REC'D	20			40
12.2.94			SALE	10	30
27.2.94			SALE	30	0

Minimum ....

Maximum ....

Re-order level ....

Re-order quantity ....

STOCK RECORD CARD

Stock Description ...30 PIECE DINNER SET...

Stock units ....

Stock Ref. No. ...5401...

Location ....10...............

Cost £9.30

DATE	GOODS RECEIVED Reference	Quantity	GOODS ISSUED Reference	Quantity	BALANCE
1-2-94	BFWD	14			14
24.2.94			SALE	2	12
20.2.94			C/SALE	4	8

Minimum ....

Maximum ....

Re-order level ....

Re-order quantity ....

STOCK RECORD CARD

Stock Description ...GOBLIN CLEANER...

Stock units ....

Stock Ref. No. ...4908...

Location ....10...............

Cost £36.75

DATE	GOODS RECEIVED Reference	Quantity	GOODS ISSUED Reference	Quantity	BALANCE
1-2-94	BFWD	7			7
2.2.94	REC'D	2			9
24.2.94			SALE	2	7
20.2.94			C/SALE	2	5

Minimum ....

Maximum ....

Re-order level ....

Re-order quantity ....

STOCK RECORD CARD

Stock Description ...12 PIECE TEA SET...

Stock units ....

Stock Ref. No. ...5402...

Location ....10...............

Cost £6.75

DATE	GOODS RECEIVED Reference	Quantity	GOODS ISSUED Reference	Quantity	BALANCE
1-2-94	BFWD	20			20
1-2-94	REC'D	10			30
18.2.94			SALE	15	15

Minimum ....

Maximum ....

Re-order level ....

Re-order quantity ....

STOCK RECORD CARD

Stock Description ...STEAM IRON...

Stock units ....

Stock Ref. No. ...4906...

Location ....10...............

Cost £14.60

DATE	GOODS RECEIVED Reference	Quantity	GOODS ISSUED Reference	Quantity	BALANCE
1-2-94	BFWD	2			2
3.2.94	REC'D	6			8
18.2.94			SALE	2	6
24.2.94			SALE	4	2
20.2.94			C/SALE	2	

Minimum ....

Maximum ....

Re-order level ....

Re-order quantity ....

STOCK RECORD CARD

Stock Description ...18 PIECE TEA SET...............................

Stock units .... Minimum ....
Stock Ref. No. ...5403........................... Maximum ....
Location ....10.................................. Re-order level ....
                                                     Re-order quantity ....

Cost £9.26

DATE	GOODS RECEIVED		GOODS ISSUED		BALANCE
	Reference	Quantity	Reference	Quantity	
1-2-94	B FWD	15			15
1-2-94	REC'D	10			25
18.2.94			SALE	5	20

STOCK RECORD CARD

Stock Description ...FOOD PROCESSOR...............................

Stock units .... Minimum ....
Stock Ref. No. ...5604........................... Maximum ....
Location ....10.................................. Re-order level ....
                                                     Re-order quantity ....

Cost £50.00

DATE	GOODS RECEIVED		GOODS ISSUED		BALANCE
	Reference	Quantity	Reference	Quantity	
1-2-94	B FWD	1			1
2.2.94	REC'D	1			2
20.2.94			C/SALE	1	1

STOCK RECORD CARD

Stock Description ...KENWOOD CHEF...............................

Stock units .... Minimum ....
Stock Ref. No. ...5601........................... Maximum ....
Location ....10.................................. Re-order level ....
                                                     Re-order quantity ....

Cost £44.00

DATE	GOODS RECEIVED		GOODS ISSUED		BALANCE
	Reference	Quantity	Reference	Quantity	
1-2-94	B FWD	14			14
2.2.94	REC'D	5			19
24.2.94			SALE	2	17

STOCK RECORD CARD

Stock Description ...KENWOOD OVEN...............................

Stock units .... Minimum ....
Stock Ref. No. ...5605........................... Maximum ....
Location ....10.................................. Re-order level ....
                                                     Re-order quantity ....

Cost £43.25

DATE	GOODS RECEIVED		GOODS ISSUED		BALANCE
	Reference	Quantity	Reference	Quantity	
1-2-94	B FWD	8			8
1-2-94	REC'D	2			10
7-2-94			SALE	2	8

STOCK RECORD CARD

Stock Description ...LIQUID ATTATCHMENT...............................

Stock units .... Minimum ....
Stock Ref. No. ...5602........................... Maximum ....
Location ....10.................................. Re-order level ....
                                                     Re-order quantity ....

Cost £10.00

DATE	GOODS RECEIVED		GOODS ISSUED		BALANCE
	Reference	Quantity	Reference	Quantity	
1-2-94	B FWD	10			10
2.2.94	REC'D	5			15
18.2.94			SALE	1	14
27.2.94			RETURN	1	13

STOCK RECORD CARD

Stock Description ...KENWOOD TOASTER...............................

Stock units .... Minimum ....
Stock Ref. No. ...5606........................... Maximum ....
Location ....10.................................. Re-order level ....
                                                     Re-order quantity ....

Cost £13.25

DATE	GOODS RECEIVED		GOODS ISSUED		BALANCE
	Reference	Quantity	Reference	Quantity	
1-2-94	B FWD	10			10
1-2-94	REC'D	10			20
18.2.94			SALE	12	8

STOCK RECORD CARD

Stock Description ...... 5 PIECE PAN SET ......

Stock units ......
Stock Ref. No. ...... 5203 ......
10
Location ......
COST £20.00

Minimum ......
Maximum ......
Re-order level ......
Re-order quantity ......

DATE	GOODS RECEIVED		GOODS ISSUED		BALANCE
	Reference	Quantity	Reference	Quantity	
1.2.94	B/FWD	0			0
2.2.94	REC'D	6			6
18.2.94			SALE	3	3

STOCK RECORD CARD

Stock Description ...... PRESSURE COOKER ......

Stock units ......
Stock Ref. No. ...... 5202 ......
10
Location ......
COST £18.66

Minimum ......
Maximum ......
Re-order level ......
Re-order quantity ......

DATE	GOODS RECEIVED		GOODS ISSUED		BALANCE
	Reference	Quantity	Reference	Quantity	
1-2-94	B FWD	0			0
1-2-94	REC'D	4			4
3.2.94	REC'D	4			8
24.2.94			SALE	2	6

STOCK RECORD CARD

Stock Description ...... KENWOOD JUG KETTLE ......

Stock units ......
Stock Ref. No. ...... 5607 ......
10
Location ......
£13.25

Minimum ......
Maximum ......
Re-order level ......
Re-order quantity ......

DATE	GOODS RECEIVED		GOODS ISSUED		BALANCE
	Reference	Quantity	Reference	Quantity	
1-2-94	B/FWD	2			2
1-2-94	REC'D	2			4
7-2-94			SALE	3	1

STOCK RECORD CARD

Stock Description ...... MINCER ......

Stock units ......
Stock Ref. No. ...... 5603 ......
10
Location ......
COST £13.50

Minimum ......
Maximum ......
Re-order level ......
Re-order quantity ......

DATE	GOODS RECEIVED		GOODS ISSUED		BALANCE
	Reference	Quantity	Reference	Quantity	
1-2-94	B FWD	0			0
2.2.94	REC'D	2			2
3.2.94	REC'D	3			5
7.2.94			SALE	5	0

Task 4

STOCK VALUATION at 28TH February 1992.

Category 1 CLOTHES.		Quantity	Cost £	Value £
0201	Three Piece Suit	46	9.10	418 60
0202	Embroidered Dress	5	5.90	29 50
0203	Beach Dress	60	4.54	272 40
0402	Pleat Front Trousers	5	5.90	29 50
0504	Brushed Cotton S/shirt	18	4.54	81 72
0505	Three Piece Office Suit	14	13.63	190 82
0704	White Bikini	22	7.00	154 00
				1176 54

Category 5 SPORTSWEAR

1001	Hang Ten Jacket	10	15.00	150 00
1002	Long John Wet Suit	10	20.00	200 00
1105	Sweatshirts	5	4.50	22 50
1106	Adidas Shorts	2	4.50	9 00
1107	Grey Sweatshirt	—	5.50	—
1108	Jog Pants	—	7.00	—
1109	Red Sweatshirt	5	8.50	42 50
1110	Blue Polo Shirts	15	5.00	75 00
1401	Pilot Fitness Shoes	15	12.50	187 50
1402	Continental Fitness Shoes	32	18.50	592 00
1403	Jack Running Shoes	35	14.00	490 00
1404	Sydney Running Shoes	—	13.00	—
				1768 50

Category 10 HOUSEHOLD

4908	Goblin Cleaner	5	36.75	183 75
4906	Steam Iron	—	14.60	—
5201	50 Pc Household Set	2	25.30	50 60
5401	30 Pc Dinner Set	8	9.30	74 40
5402	12 Pc Tea Set	15	6.75	101 25
5403	18 Pc Tea Set	20	9.25	185 00
5601	Kenwood Chef	17	66.00	1122 00
5602	Liquid Attachment	13	10.00	130 00
5604	Food Processor	1	50.00	50 00
5605	Kenwood Oven	8	43.25	346 00
5606	Kenwood Toaster	8	13.25	106 00
5603	Mincer	—	13.50	—
5607	Kenwood Jug Kettle	1	13.25	13 25
5202	Pressure Cooker	6	18.66	111 96
5203	5 Pc Pan Set	3	20.00	60 00
				2534 21

Unit VIII Solutions

Task 1

VAT CONTROL ACCOUNT

			Inputs Tax	£			Outputs Tax	£
					Jan	1	balance b/fwd	230 72
Jan	31	Purchases P/0/8	1112 79		Jan	31	Returns Out R/0/8	4 07
Jan	31	Returns In R/1/8	6 61		Jan	31	Sales S/7/B	1498 11
Jan	31	Petty Cash P/c	16 02		Jan	31	Cash Sales P/c	142 50
Jan	31	Expenses	111 56					
Jan	31	Balance c/dwn	628 42					
			1875 40					1875 40
					Feb	1	Balance b/fwd	628 42

Task 2

		Unit (6)			
		Petty Cash Sales			
Jan	18	Sports for All 82	71	69	
Jan	28	Tamworth Fash 83	70	81	
			142	50	

		Unit (7)			
		Expences			
Jan	25	Electricity Board	26	00	
Jan	31	B'ham Even Herald	23	12	
Jan	30	Adam Ford	34	49	
Jan	31	Tamworth Svar	9	42	
Jan	20	Adam Ford	16	82	
Jan	17	Print on Front	1	71	
			111	56	

		Unit (6)			
		Petty Cash VAT	16	02	

Deductions Working Sheet P11   Year to 5 April 19 ___   *[EXTRA*

Employer's name	*Family favourites*
Tax District and reference	*FF 464/327*

Complete only for occupational pension schemes newly contracted-out since January 1986.
Scheme contracted-out number

S	4						

Employee's surname *in CAPITALS*	SIMS	First two forenames	ROGER BRIAN

National Insurance no.	Date of birth *in figures* Day Month Year	Works no. etc	Date of leaving *in figu...* Day Month Yea
ZM 10 62 71 A	29 12 48	01	

Tax code †	525 H	Amended code †			
		Wk/Mth in which applied			

Month no	Week no	Pay in the week or month including Statutory Sick Pay/Statutory Maternity pay 2	Total pay to date 3	Total free pay to date (Table A) 4a	K codes only Total 'additional pay' to date (Table A) 4b	Total taxable pay to date i.e. column 3 *minus* column 4a or column 3 *plus* column 4b 5	Total tax due to date as shown by Taxable Pay Tables 6	Tax due at end of current period. Mark refunds 'R' 6a	Regulatory limit i.e. 50% of column 2 entry 6b	Tax deducted or refunded the week or month. Mark refunds 'R' 7
Bt fwd	Bt fwd	£	£	£	£	£	£	£	£	£
11	47	712 00	8637 60	4829 11		3808 49	837 41			
12	52	1062 00	9699 60	5268 12		4431 48	982 75			145 3

9699 | 60 ◄	**Pay and Tax totals** Previous employments ►
◄	This employment *Mark net refund 'R'* ►

982 | 75

Where you are us... K code enter total ... amounts in column... employment

National Insurance contributions

For employer's use	Earnings on which employee's contributions payable 1a	Earnings on which employee's and employer's contributions payable 1b	Employee's contributions payable 1c	Earnings on which employee's contributions at contracted-out rate payable included in column 1c 1d	Employee's contributions at contracted-out rate included in column 1c 1e	Statutory Sick Pay in the week or month included in column 2 1f	Statutory Sick Pay recovered. Only complete this if you are claiming Small Employer's Relief. 1g	Statutory Maternity Pay in the week or month included in column 2 1h	Month no
	Bt £ fwd	Bt £ fwd	Bt £ fwd	Bt £ fwd	Bt £ fwd	Bt £ fwd	Bt £ fwd	Bt £ fwd	Bt fwd
bfwd	8637	1332 65	590 04						11
		188 82	78 48						12
		1521 41	668 52						
						▲ SSP total		▲ SMP total	

Index